PRESENTATION THINKING & DESIGN

Create better presentations, quicker

ED GRUWEZ

PEARSON

Harlow, England • London • New York • Boston • San Francisco • Toronto • Sydney
Auckland • Singapore • Hong Kong • Tokyo • Seoul • Taipei • New Delhi
Cape Town • São Paulo • Mexico City • Madrid • Amsterdam • Munich • Paris • Milan

PEARSON EDUCATION LIMITED

Edinburgh Gate
Harlow CM20 2JE
United Kingdom
Tel: +44 (0)1279 623623
Web: www.pearson.com/uk

First published 2014 (print and electronic)

© Gedecom NV 2014 (print and electronic)

Pearson Education is not responsible for the content of third-party internet sites.

ISBN: 978-1-292-01357-2 (print)
        978-1-292-01587-3 (PDF)
        978-1-292-01359-6 (ePub)
        978-1-292-01358-9 (eText)

British Library Cataloguing-in-Publication Data
A catalogue record for the print edition is available from the British Library

Library of Congress Cataloging-in-Publication Data
Gruwez, Ed.
  Presentation thinking and design : create better presentations, quicker / Ed Gruwez.
    pages cm
  Includes bibliographical references and index.
  ISBN 978-1-292-01357-2
  1. Business presentations. I. Title.
  HF5718.22.G78 2014
  658.4'52--dc23

                    2014024808

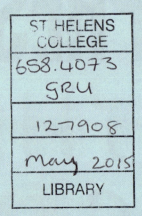

The screenshots in this book are reprinted by permission of Microsoft Corporation.

10 9 8 7 6 5 4 3 2 1
18 17 16 15 14

Cover design by Dan Mogford
Text design by Design Deluxe
Illustrations by Ed Gruwez
Slides by Ed Gruwez and Kris Geluykens

Print edition typeset in 9.5pt Helvetica Neue LT Pro by 3
Print edition printed by Ashford Colour Press Ltd, Gosport

NOTE THAT ANY PAGE CROSS REFERENCES REFER TO THE PRINT EDITION

Praise for Presentation Thinking and Design

'Do you spend a lot of time at work sitting through really poor presentations? Do you wish you were more effective at getting your ideas across? If so, this is the book for you. Ed Gruwez has developed a simple and compelling framework for helping you design and deliver your presentation, and he also explains *why* his ideas make sense. However skilled you think you are, I guarantee this book will help you to become a better presenter.'

JULIAN BIRKINSHAW, PROFESSOR, LONDON BUSINESS SCHOOL

'The art lies in its simplicity! Ed is a master in his approach to design content.'

FRANCIS PEENE, DIRECTOR, CHANGE BANK FOR THE FUTURE PROGRAM, BNP PARIBAS FORTIS

'This outstanding book will revolutionise the way you think about and execute presentations. The insights will maximise your impact!'

PHILLIP VANDERVOORT, GENERAL MANAGER, MARKETING AND OPERATIONS LATIN AMERICA, MICROSOFT

'Finally there is a book to reveal the easiest and most powerful way to get presentations right. In fact, it is not just about presentation, but also about transforming complex concepts into a set of crisp and compelling messages, which is essential for anyone who needs to communicate across a big organisation. A must read!'

I FEN CHIANG, GLOBAL DIRECTOR, COMMERCIAL EXCELLENCE, NUTRICIA

'Ed Gruwez's book is a must read. It helps any level in the organisation develop neat and impactful presentations, but also brings a breakthrough approach on slideshow productivity.'

NICOLAS FILATIEFF, DIRECTOR, MARKETING CLIENTS AND PRODUCTS, BNP PARIBAS FORTIS

'I saw a clear uplift in presentation quality after we used Ed's support to educate and train our teams. The presentations became crisper, shorter, to the point and impactful. And the caviar is that the team members really enjoyed the training and acknowledged that it helped them create and deliver presentations in a better way.'

FLORENT EDOUARD, SENIOR DIRECTOR, COMMERCIAL EXCELLENCE, ASTRAZENECA JAPAN

'TNS's mission is to consult business and policy leaders and help them to make better decisions. Reporting and presenting our research findings, insights, conclusions and recommendations with impact have become the key success criteria for valuing our service. The 'TLSM' approach allowed us to work in a more efficient and structured way, resulting in more effective research presentations and reports.'

DOMINIQUE VERCRAEYE, MANAGING DIRECTOR, TNS BELGIUM

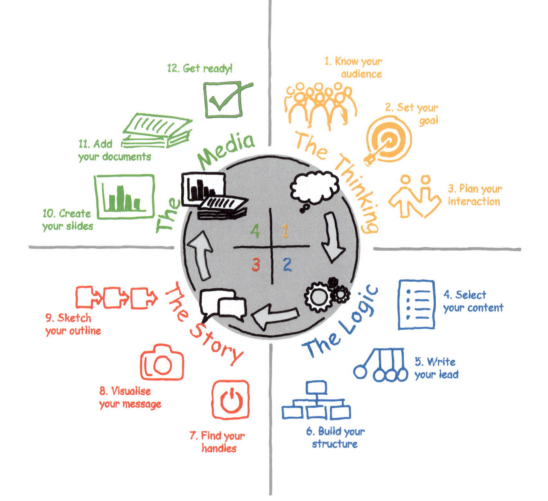

Contents

About the author

Edouard Gruwez, MSc, MBA was born in 1962. He was marketing and business development director for GM and Volvo before becoming managing director of Ogilvy Internal Communications in 2004. As a consultant, he works mainly on internal communications, transformation and employee engagement in large organisations.

In 2010 he started to develop a method to help managers design better presentations in less time, driven by his clients' frustration with the quality of presentations. The method proved to be such a success, that he continued to develop it further and backed it up with solid scientific research.

With his company, To The Point At Work Ltd (www.tothepointatwork.com), he helps organisations to become much more efficient in the way they work and communicate. He now lectures about the subject of designing presentations and digital communication and he is a frequent speaker at conferences. He has trained hundreds of managers, coached senior executives and globally helped companies to change their communication culture.

Acknowledgements

This book is based on the insights acquired during years of practical experience as a manager, consultant and designer of presentations. But without the input of numerous other people, it would have been impossible for me to translate this practical experience into this book. Much of the content has been gathered from dozens of books and more than 200 scientific articles. As a result, it is sometimes difficult to know which idea came from which source. My apologies if unintentionally I fail to mention one of these sources. You will find a list of references at the end of the book and a more detailed list on my website **www.edgruwez.com**.

In addition, I would also like to thank my colleagues, friends, family, principals and trainees for their valuable contributions to the writing of the book. I am deeply grateful to them all.

First and foremost, my three children: Valentine, Henri and Arthur.

But also the following people, who provided their help and support: André Sainderichin, Kaat Vanseer, Dominique Vercraeye, Charlyne Mercier, Christian Dekoninck, Clara Edouard, Frank Momoth, Geert Serneels, Ian Connerty, Glenn Vissenaekens, Graham Darracott, Joep Paemen, Jacques Gruwez, Johan De Pelsmaker, Jordi Kastelijn, Julian Birkinshaw, Karin Vermeiren, Kris Geluykens, Manu De Cort, Nicole Eggleton, Paul Van Damme, Peter Saerens, Sylvie Verleye, Philip Vyt, Tim Smits, Tim Van der Schraelen, Joey Stoole and Vanessa Stoole.

PUBLISHER'S ACKNOWLEDGEMENTS

The publisher is grateful to the following for permission to reproduce copyright material:

Figure on page 53 adapted from Herrmann, N., *The Whole Brain Business Book: Unlocking the power of whole brain thinking in organizations and individuals*, © 1996, published by McGraw-Hill Education. Reproduced with permission of McGraw-Hill Education; Table on page 176 adapted from tables 14.1, 14.2 and 14.3 (pages 267–268) in Richard E Mayer, *Multimedia Learning*, 2nd Edition, © Richard E Mayer 2001, 2009, published by Cambridge University Press, adapted with permission.

The publisher would also like to thank the following for their kind permission to reproduce their photographs:

Shutterstock.com:
Page 61: Talvi (top panel); defpicture (bottom panel). **Page 146:** Dmitry Lobanov (top left panel); michaeljung (top right panel: woman); Gelpi JM (top right panel: man); Jeroen van den Broek

(centre left panel); dibrova (centre right panel); Zack Frank (bottom left panel); Dan Kosmayer (bottom right panel: ice cream sundaes); KIM NGUYEN (bottom right panel: sugared biscuits); Hong Vo (bottom right panel: iced doughnuts); Matthew Cole (bottom right panel: chicken nuggets); michelaubryphoto (bottom right panel: fast food meal). **Page 165:** Carsten Reisinger. **Page 169:** Ljupco Smokovski (top left panel: woman on bike); Andresr (top right panel: man); Sarunyu_foto (top right panel: green earth); Hluboki Dzianis (top right panel: cityscape); spaxiax (bottom panel: heartbeat); Andresr (bottom panel: man and woman); dandoo (bottom panel: clock); Andresr (bottom panel: family of four). **Page 170:** zentilia (bottom right panel: car). **Page 171:** Rob Wilson (top right panel: bus). **Page 175:** Orhan Cam. **Page 183:** Pressmaster (top right panel); Monkey Business Images (bottom panels). **Page 184:** Betacam-SP. **Page 187:** dotshock (basketball player photograph); Svetlana Chebanova (bottom left panel: basketball player silhouette); EDHAR (bottom left panel: handshake); NAS CRETIVES (bottom right panel: female first aider). **Page 189:** BlueSkyImage.

The PowerPoint screenshots in this book are reprinted by permission of Microsoft Corporation, Gedecom NV and Slidedesigners BVBA.

All cartoon illustrations © Gedecom NV.

Every effort has been made to trace the copyright holders and we apologise in advance for any unintentional omissions. We would be pleased to insert the appropriate acknowledgement in any subsequent edition of this publication.

Note concerning the examples: there are numerous examples included in the book. Although they are all based on real life experience, the names and details have been changed often to respect confidentiality. As for the slides, they serve only as an illustration of the principles. The information within the slides should not be regarded as fact – any resemblance to existing material is purely coincidental.

Introduction

In 2010 Johan De Pelsmaker, a director at BNP Paribas Fortis, asked me to find a training course for his department at the bank's headquarters. All the participants were high-flyers and all of them had followed training on presentation delivery previously. But Johan was looking for something more and had clear ideas on the matter. He wanted training that zoomed in on the content of a presentation, not the presentation delivery. What do I put in? How do I structure it? How do I make it effective and memorable? He wanted to ensure that his team would stand head and shoulders above the rest.

I was keen to help him, but was unable to find a single trainer on the market who could provide exactly what Johan was looking for. I couldn't even find a book or method that came close to what Johan wanted.

Because presentations are close to my heart, eventually I decided to give the training myself. I ploughed my way through the available literature, added my own experience and designed a process to build presentations. The reactions exceeded all expectations.

Participants said that this training dramatically improved the effectiveness of their presentations. As time passed, gradually I refined this method, based on the experiences of the many hundreds of people who took part in the training programmes, supplemented with research findings.

Two years later, after I had presented the method at the London Business School, it was suggested that it would be a good idea to share these insights in a book. This is that book.

JUST ANOTHER BOOK ABOUT PRESENTATIONS?

As a consultant, I visit organisations in many different sectors of the economy: banking, telecoms, consumer goods, pharmaceuticals, even government organisations. And one thing that strikes me is the huge number of slides that people are producing each day.

At the same time, I see how difficult it is to put together a logically constructed, interesting and convincing presentation. This difficulty is one of the reasons why I am called in by these organisations. Many managers feel that sub-standard presentations are responsible for loss of time, unnecessary irritation and bad decision making. This is surprising, since a presentation easily can be made to the point: concise but complete, convincing, motivating and even entertaining.

Many excellent books have been written already on the subject. Unfortunately, most of them confine themselves to tips and tricks for the delivery of presentations and often focus on presentations for large audiences; what I call keynote presentations. The reality of most business presentations is quite different.

Keynote

The usual business presentation

Walk through the corridors of any office building and peek into the meeting rooms. Almost everywhere you will find a presentation in progress. Usually for a limited audience. For specialists, customers, colleagues, etc. With a wide range of objectives: selling, convincing, warning, preparing decisions, presenting strategies, starting projects, training personnel, etc.

This book has been written first and foremost for people who need to give or design presentations in a business context – although keynote speakers also might find inspiration in the following pages.

The focus is not on the presentation delivery, but rather on the content and preparation work that precedes the delivery. Right from the very beginning, a blank sheet of paper, up to the moment when you draw that deep breath before you begin to speak.

The success of your presentation depends entirely on that preparation. If your presentation is carefully designed – in accordance with 'the rules of the game' – it will run like clockwork. If you are well prepared, you no longer need to act a role when you are presenting; instead, you can just be yourself and focus fully on your audience.

WHY IS THIS BOOK DIFFERENT?

This book differs from what you find in many other books about presentations in five ways:

1 **A scientific basis.** This book is a practical book. But it is based on scientific insights. You will see regular references to research that support the book's arguments and you will find more information on the website **www.edgruwez.com**.

2 **Focus on reason and logic.** It is unquestionable that human beings are, first and foremost, emotional creatures. But there is more to communication than the emotional side. Faulty reasoning and poor structure can never be made good with a flood of enthusiastic words, wrapped up in emotional packaging. This book keeps the right balance between reason and emotion.

3 **Perfection versus speed.** With the method proposed in this book, you will be able to reduce the time you need to prepare your presentation, but without harming the quality of the end product.

4 **A structured approach.** To make a good presentation, you need to think about a hundred different things all at the same time. Framing your presentation design within a structured process makes things much easier.

5 **Complete.** Rather than giving a selection of tips, this book attempts to give a complete overview. You don't need to read everything, read those things that are most relevant to you.

HOW IS THIS BOOK STRUCTURED?

The book is divided into two parts.

Part I offers a number of important insights, starting with the presentation paradox. This is followed by an explanation of good and bad presentations. This, in turn, requires a minimal understanding of the way our brains work. These scientific insights will help you to design better presentations, and clarify the logic of the TLSM method.

Part II takes you in detail through the four phases necessary to construct your presentation. And you will be given plenty of practical tips to help you to transform the theoretical insights into usable ideas.

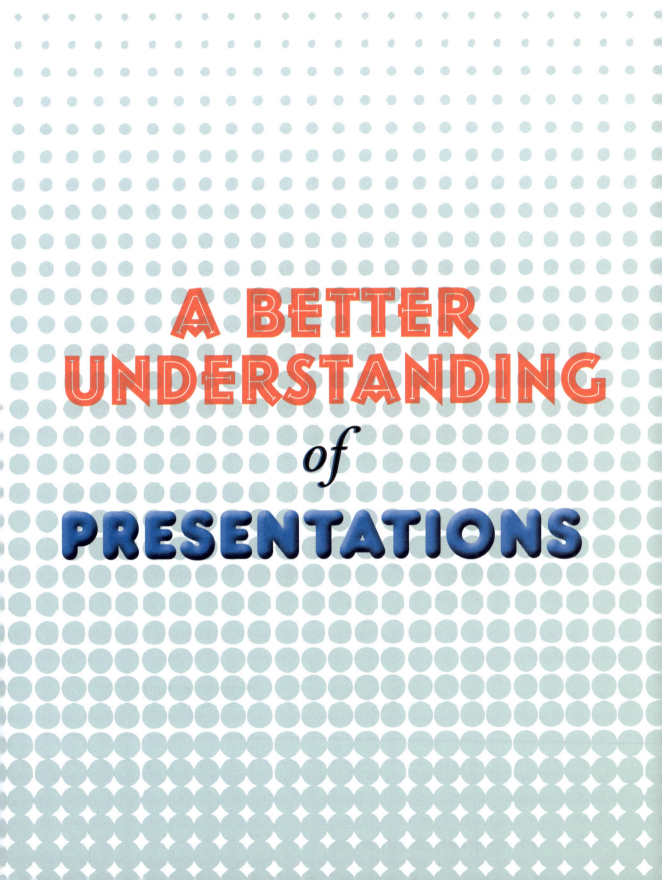

The presentation paradox

There is something odd about presentations. On the one hand, we can't live without them. They are an almost ever-present part of day-to-day business life. Presentations are often the cornerstone of debate and discussion. They form an important part of the strategic planning process. And they are a critical part of business communication. On the other hand, there are not many people who actually would admit to liking the presentations that are being produced. They are often painfully long, visually unattractive and boring as hell and everyone complains that they lose too much time and use too much energy making slides. Some even doubt the efficiency of presentations as a communication tool. Certain CEOs and authors have gone so far as to describe PowerPoint as an assault on intellectual thought. Slides lead a life of their own and detract from the processes of dialogue, interaction and reflection – or so they say. Presentations are both a blessing and a curse.

Presentation paradox
Hate or love ?

WHAT, ACTUALLY, IS A PRESENTATION?

I began my career with General Motors. My boss was a man named Dan Young. He was a full-blooded New Yorker and used his undoubted charisma to get the best out of his team. Even though he was a born presenter, he preferred giving us the chance to show what we could do, rather than standing in the spotlight himself. He allowed me to give presentations regularly, which in turn allowed me to develop my presentational skills.

Years later, when I was working at another company in a much more senior position, my team was chosen to present an important strategic project. My boss asked me if I would make the presentation. I did so, with great energy and enthusiasm. I made sure that the content was iron-strong and that the visuals were impressive. Nothing could go wrong, or so I thought ... So, imagine my surprise when my boss informed me the day before the meeting that he intended to give the presentation using my slides! For him, 'making a presentation' meant little more than 'making a slide deck'.

Let's get this straight before we go any further: a presentation is much more than just a slide deck. A presentation is a happening. It involves an individual speaking to a group of people about a specific subject, using support materials to emphasise the message. And, yes, one of the most common supporting materials is, indeed, slides. But not always!

or   or

What is a presentation?

The term 'powerpoint' often leads to misunderstanding. So, let me set matters straight. PowerPoint is a program and trademark of the Microsoft Corporation.

You use PowerPoint to design slides. But it is by no means the only software you can use. Keynote, Prezi, Google Slides or Open Office are some of the alternatives. However, the Microsoft program of the same name has become so commonplace that the product it generates is now also known by the term 'powerpoint'. Just like the generic term 'aspirin' evolved from what was originally a brand name.

To avoid confusion, in this book I use 'PowerPoint' whenever I refer to the software and 'powerpoint' as a term to describe a set of presentation slides, usually referred to as a slide deck.

PRESENTATIONS ARE A BLESSING

A few months ago I was working with my colleagues on a pitch for a new client. The client's representative, Anne, told us that she did not want any presentations from her service providers – in this case, us. The provision of an electronic document was sufficient, she said. And so we sent her a 10-page document. To write it and polish it up took a little over a day. To read it probably took 20 minutes.

Anne phoned to say that it was an interesting document, but there were still one or two points that were not fully clear. Even after she had read the document three times. Perhaps we could call in and explain things to her?

A few days later we presented the same story to Anne and five of her colleagues. We made just 10 slides for this presentation, which lasted 20 minutes, followed by a 20-minute question and answer session.

Afterwards, all the participants said they found the presentation interesting and, above all, crystal-clear – even those who had never had the chance to read the original 10-page document ...

When you use a presentation well, it is by far the best way to communicate a complex subject. What's more, it saves time – and both the 'sender' and the 'receiver' benefit.

1 **You get immediate feedback.** You are in direct contact with your audience. You can see immediately if people don't understand what you mean or don't agree with what you say, and you can adjust your communication continually.

2 **You communicate in a natural way.** Talking with an audience and making use of visual aids is a natural form of communication. Research suggests that this leads to more efficient communication than sending written documents (media naturalness theory).

3 **You have eye contact.** Numerous research studies have confirmed the importance of eye contact and body language in communication. We understand each other better when we can look into each other's eyes and see each other's facial expressions.

4 **Effective use of time.** A presentation allows you to communicate larger amounts of information in a given time than most other communication channels (see Dual channel approach in Solution 1, page 26).

PRESENTATIONS ARE A CURSE

I once did a survey of a hundred or so managers. I asked them what they thought of the presentations they saw currently in their daily work. This was by no means a 'scientific' survey, but it brought some interesting facts to light. The most striking conclusion was that most of the managers thought that the majority of presentations were no good. Here are some of my questions and the average answers.

1	How many presentations have you watched during the past week?	7.4
2	How many of those presentations had no added value whatsoever?	37%
3	How many of those presentations did you think were bad?	71% (of which 25% were really bad)

Source: Gruwez and Vanseer, 2014

I agree with them that most presentations given in a business environment are of an appalling quality. And, actually, they are even more inefficient and ineffective than most managers think.

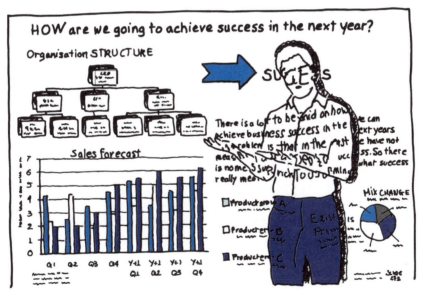

Presentations can be a curse

What are the consequences?

Bad presentations can cause a lot of irritation, waste and harm.

- Lack of effective results.
- Wasted time during the preparation and successive correction rounds.
- Wasted time and frustration of the presenter, who fails to achieve the results he expected.
- The subject cannot be worked through, so it keeps reappearing on the agenda of subsequent meetings.
- Annoyance with the audience, who feel they are losing time and whose thoughts are elsewhere (sending SMSs, reading their emails, flicking through documents, etc.).
- Crossed wires in communication, because the participants drown in a flood of details.

But, perhaps, the most serious consequence of all is the cost. Follow, if you will, the calculation that I made recently for one of my clients. About 1,000 people work in the company's head office. Each month, about 1,000 presentations are made. This equates to about 30,000 slides. Staff spend about 15,000 hours preparing these slides and the audiences spend about 30,000 hours looking at them and listening to the speakers. If you can reduce preparation time by 15 per cent and the presentation length by 20 per cent, you can save 8,250 hours per month – at the drop of a hat! Add to this additional profit, because the resulting decisions are better, taken more quickly and action plans are implemented with greater speed and efficiency. And this is before we mention the reduction of irritation and frustration in the company as a whole. Who can put a price on that?

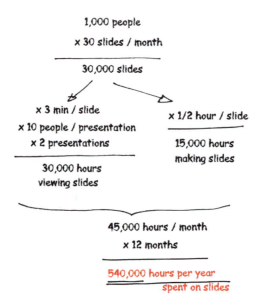

1,000 people

x 30 slides / month

30,000 slides

x 3 min / slide
x 10 people / presentation
x 2 presentations

30,000 hours
viewing slides

x 1/2 hour / slide

15,000 hours
making slides

45,000 hours / month
x 12 months

540,000 hours per year
spent on slides

WHAT CAUSES THE PROBLEM?

There are many causes for bad presentations. Most boil down to these two:

1 Presentations are difficult to create.

2 Most presentations are poorly prepared.

1 Presentations are difficult to create

The sheer quantity of communication is too great

Since the arrival of electronic media, we are all suffering from a communication overload. None of us is capable of reading and processing all the messages we receive. And this bombardment is increasing in scale every day. It is like trying to quench your thirst by drinking from a fire hose.

Communication in the twenty-first century...

... is like drinking from a fire hose

The total mass of information received by people is estimated at 100,500 words per day. This is equivalent to two books of 250 pages. And this amount increases by 4.4 per cent per year or an equivalent of 50 per cent every 10 years!

This brings us to a second paradox: notwithstanding the massive flood of information people are continually complaining about ... a lack of information! The reason is simple: our brains simply are not capable of registering and recording everything we see, read or hear. This means that much of the information on offer falls on stony ground.

Does this mean that you can approach your subject only superficially? Perhaps. But really good presentations are both concise and complete. It is a very difficult trade-off, but perfectly possible.

Presentations are a complex means of communication

In most forms of communication there is only one 'sender' and one 'receiver', linked by a single channel of communication. This is the case with books, emails, reports, websites, phones, etc. Often there is also a form of feedback, when the sender and the receiver briefly change roles.

But, in most presentations, you make use of supporting material as well, such as your slides. In this way, a 'triangular relationship' is created. The audience has two information sources: the speaker and his slides. And, as speaker, you also interact with the audience and your slides. The communication resulting from a presentation is much richer and more efficient than, say, an email. But, at the same time, it is more complex and thus more difficult to do well.

Presenting is triangular communication

We all underestimate the difficulty of communication

Communicating something complex in a simple manner is very difficult. Take this book, for example. As an author, I want to give you, my readers, the benefit of my insights. These insights are crystal clear in my own mind. But how can I be sure that they are just as clear in your mind?

Think of it as an image, as a photo you have in your mind, that you want to implant into the memory of someone else. To transmit this image, first you need to cut it into pieces. Next, you encode each piece with appropriate words. These words then are fired off at the reader. All you can now do is hope that they decode the words in the manner you want and connect them in the right way to reconstruct the image you intended.

The curse of knowledge

A fundamental problem is that transmission of knowledge always takes place against the background of the teller's own knowledge. A speaker generally knows his subject well and knows what he wants to say. The problem is that, because of his knowledge, the speaker is incapable of seeing how his words come across to someone who doesn't have that knowledge.

A test conducted by Elizabeth Newton at Stanford University illustrates this (Newton, 1990; Heath & Heath, 2006). A group of people were given the task of clapping out the rhythm of a popular song. They could choose from a list of 25 titles. Other participants in the test were given the same list of songs and were asked to identify the melodies being clapped. Just 2.5 per cent of the songs were recognised. Perhaps this is not so surprising. Much more surprising is that the clappers were convinced that 50 per cent of the songs they had clapped would be recognised easily by the listeners. Talk about self-overestimation!

We communicate as though we are talking to ourselves. Everything that someone says is perfectly logical for that person and so he fails to understand that the people listening to him hear something different from what he thinks he is saying. They interpret his words in their own way. This allows errors to creep into our communication, which undermine the message we are trying to project. The image that the listener has in his head is not the same as the image transmitted by the teller. And, because it is impossible for us to get inside someone else's head, the only way to be sure that your message has been received in the right way is to ask for feedback.

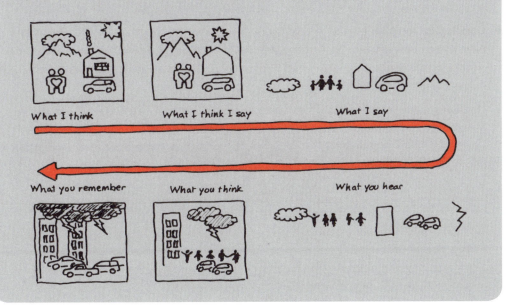

What I think

What I think I say

What I say

What you remember

What you think

What you hear

'I know that you believe you understand what you think I said, but I'm not sure you realise that what you heard is not what I meant.' Robert McCloskey, writer and illustrator

2 Most presentations are poorly prepared

I am not pretending that I know everything about good and bad presentations. But, based on my experience of the hundreds of presenters I have trained and the thousands of presentations I have seen, I can at least offer the following list of most frequently made mistakes in preparing a presentation:

- **Lack of reflection.** How much time do you take to think about a presentation before you actually start making slides? Most people can answer that question easily: none. They begin immediately with their slides. But the less time you spend in preparatory thought, the more problems you are going to have later on. You will lose more time in correcting, amending and reordering your slides. And with all this reorganisation, the structure of your presentation often will be weak and difficult to follow.

- **Too many details.** The fear of many presenters is incompleteness. And so they cram their presentations full with details. Just to be on the safe side. This results in overloaded presentations that lose the audience long before the end.

- **Too long.** It is really irritating when 30 minutes are allocated for a presentation, but the presenter arrives with 40 or more slides. After half an hour he is only half way through. He runs over time and needs to improvise a rushed ending that leaves the audience with the wrong message.

- **Conclusion too late.** In most presentations the conclusion comes at the end. Presenters often begin with too much background, followed by too much detailed analysis. They get around to their conclusion – the most important bit – only when time is running out and most people's attention has long since flown.

- **Unclear message.** And what is that conclusion? What is it you want to say? Ask that question to a presenter and listen to his answers. If he launches into a long or incoherent explanation, then you know that he is poorly prepared. What is the point of a presentation if the speaker doesn't know what he wants to achieve?

- **Too quick to opt for PowerPoint.** To save time, most presenters opt to design their presentation directly in PowerPoint or some other presentation software. This has some negative side-effects:

  - **The wrong order.** If you start making a powerpoint immediately, you put down the information in the order in which it comes into your head. But that is seldom the right order for your audience to understand the message easily.

- **Bad content.** When you make slides in PowerPoint, your focus is on the software: 'How can I make a circle?', 'How do I align that photo?', 'Oh, no, the bullets have disappeared; how do I get them back?' If you are too busy wrestling with the intricacies of PowerPoint, you may have a presentation that is a graphic masterpiece – but the content sucks.

- **Not critical enough.** If you have spent a long time working on your powerpoint, it is difficult to be critical about the end result. Everything looks great! You are not going to delete that beautiful slide that took you an hour to make, are you?

• **Slides for the speaker instead of the public.** Many speakers are frightened of having a black-out. And so they make their slides for themselves. Everything they want to say is on the slides, sometimes even full sentences! This leads to overfull slides, which defeats the object of the exercise. Who is going to listen to a presenter if you can read everything he says on the screen?

• **Bad habits are contagious.** Young managers often tell me how, as 'new boys', they are surprised by the poor quality of the presentations in their company. But, just years later, they have adopted the habit of their colleagues and bosses to produce the same bad, overloaded presentations. Changing a presentation culture proves to be a difficult thing.

So, if senior managers complain about presentation quality, probably they should look into their own hearts first. Presentation quality is a shared responsibility between the presenter, his audience and his manager.

• **Too much of a good thing.** Occasionally I see a 'theatrical' presentation. Some speakers try to turn their presentation into a show, as though they are the reincarnation of Steve Jobs. But, too many unexpected twists, too fancy slides or too many jokes are often a cover-up for a lack of content. It's like disguising a piece of bad meat under a spicy sauce. The meat is still bad!

- **Insufficient knowledge of the software.** A lot of time is wasted because presenters don't really know how to use their presentation software. Managers lose countless hours messing about with slides – hours that could be used much better elsewhere.

As you can see, there is a whole range of mistakes that lead to bad presentations. And bad presentations have serious consequences that always are totally underestimated.

It's all the fault of PowerPoint!

In 2010 the *New York Times* told the story of General Stanley McChrystal, who was shown a powerpoint about the American strategy in Afghanistan (Bumiller, 2010). One slide bore an alarming resemblance to a plate of spaghetti. McChrystal exclaimed: 'When we understand this slide, we will have won the war.' The whole room burst out laughing. The slide went viral and was soon a source of amusement around the world. But, at the same time, the incident hid a more serious point. General McChrystal later said: 'It (powerpoint) is dangerous because it creates the illusion that we control and understand everything. But some of the world's problems can't be reduced to a handful of "bullets".'

Critics of PowerPoint claim that the program does more harm than good. It prevents critical thinking, hinders decision making and is so widely used that it has become almost an epidemic. The poor Microsoft program is blamed for all the sins of the world!

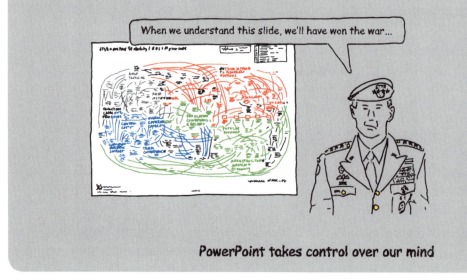

PowerPoint takes control over our mind

PowerPoint certainly strengthens the tendency to communicate in a fragmented, high-level way. Many details are lost, so that it is possible to misread vital information. But is this really the fault of PowerPoint? Personally, I don't think so. I do, however, agree with the claim that bad slides lead to bad decisions.

In defence of PowerPoint

In his essay 'In Defense of PowerPoint', Don Norman wrote: 'The problem is with the talk, not with the tool.' (Norman, 2004).

Even before the advent of PowerPoint, many presentations were boring and disappointing. And, yes, it is certainly true that PowerPoint influences the way in which we present and think. There is an inherent tendency to fragment ideas and provoke cognitive overload. Slides with long lists are not suitable for communicating complex material. But this is not the program's fault. When used properly, PowerPoint has shown itself to be a valuable tool. So, perhaps our judgement should be more balanced.

Research has shown that, when used properly, the tool itself has little effect on the quality of the end result. This is as true for PowerPoint as for every other digital presentation medium. Some people swear by newer tools, such as Prezi. However, research by Jordi Casteleyn has demonstrated that, if the slides are well designed, it doesn't really matter what software you use. Programs like Prezi, which work with an 'infinite canvas', initially attract people's attention better. But, once the novelty has worn off, they do not result in a better recall or understanding of the presentation (Casteleyn, 2013).

Final conclusion? If you feel comfortable using PowerPoint, no problem. Just carry on using the tool you know best. But make sure that your slides and your presentation are 100 per cent in order!

Slides as a tool for knowledge production and transfer

In her 2011 article about strategy and PowerPoint, Sarah Kaplan underlines the important role of slides in developing and imparting strategic knowledge (Kaplan, 2011). She explains how PowerPoint simplifies the difficult task of negotiating and giving meaning in a complex and uncertain context. PowerPoint creates room for discussion, makes possible the recombination of knowledge, allows ideas to be amended as they evolve, and helps to communicate relevant knowledge to a selected range of actors. In other words, PowerPoint here is seen as a work instrument rather than a presentation instrument.

This is certainly true. I have often seen strategies develop step by step, with slides being amended in each successive version. Senior managers use these slides to reach decisions and to discuss specific issues. Slides are short, concise, easy to share and easy to change. They are a great way to distil and communicate ideas before actually putting them down on paper.

However, slides that are generated in this manner usually are far too complex to be used in a presentation.

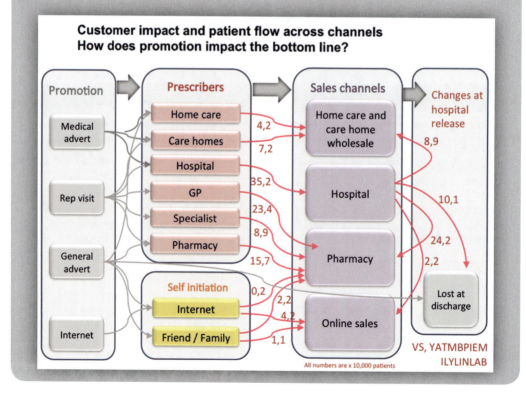

HOW TO MAKE BETTER PRESENTATIONS

My uncle, Jacques Gruwez, is a well-known Professor Emeritus and was a surgeon before he retired. He lectured in surgery and was head of the surgery department at the university hospital. He is a talented speaker and a popular guest at worldwide congresses and seminars. In short, he is someone to look up to, someone from whom you can seek advice. And, so, I asked him once what his secret was for a good presentation. He smiled and answered: 'A good presentation should be like a mini skirt: as short as possible to catch everyone's attention, and just long enough to cover what it needs to cover.'

Uncle Jacques admitted that this metaphor was originally one of Churchill's. Like most of his quotes, it is witty and amusing, but it also summarises the essence of the matter: short, but complete. Talking in public – oratory – has been praised as an art since ancient times. The famous orator Marcus Fabius Quintilianus listed five important characteristics of a good orator:

1 Focus on the feelings of the audience.

2 Show good character and benevolent spirit.

3 Use emotions to strengthen your message.

4 Be moved by your own message.

5 Use imagery that touches a chord with the audience.

The old Roman insights are still valid today, but perhaps we can add one or two more elements to the list. So, what makes a really good twenty-first-century presentation?

1 It achieves the objectives of the speaker.

2 It is concise but complete.

3 It is clear, logically structured and easy to understand.

4 It attracts and keeps attention.

5 It is relevant for the audience.

6 It is entertaining and makes a good impression.

7 It not only engages the mind but also touches the heart.

Good news

It sounds like a cliché but, if I didn't believe it, this book would have no point: the art of making good presentations can be learnt! You really can turn yourself into a better presenter. And, as presentations are by far the strongest form of communication in business environments, I would advise you to invest some time in them. With a little methodology, insight and practice, soon you will be making much better presentations in less time.

You don't need to be a born orator to make a good presentation. My company sometimes organises events for our clients where a number of speakers take part. Frequently, the client asks the audience to assess the speakers: How did you like the presentation? Not surprisingly, the most fluent and entertaining speakers usually get the best scores. But what does it really tell you? I prefer to ask the audience what they most remember about what was said.

You will be surprised by the result. More than 75 per cent of all messages are lost in the delivery. What's more – and this is the good news for most of us who aren't born orators – there is no correlation at all between the speaker's eloquence and the audience's ability to remember the message.

Chip and Dan Heath (speakers and co-authors) have provided the scientific evidence to back up this claim. They carried out an experiment at Stanford University in which they asked a number of students to give a one-minute presentation (Heath & Heath, 2007). Other students were asked to assess these presentations. As you might expect, Stanford has no shortage of good and intelligent speakers. And, as in our example above, the best and most fluent speakers were given the highest scores. Foreign students scored worst, because of their poorer command of the English language. But, when people were asked to write down what they had remembered most from the presentations, the results were very different. The disparity between the American and the foreign students disappeared entirely. In other words, the ability to remember something depends on the content and the structure of the presentation; it has little to do with the eloquence of the speaker.

Boost your creative thinking

Many managers I meet say that they are not creative or that their subject does not lend itself to creativity. Neither of these statements is true. We are all creative beings and we all have the ability to practise and improve our creativity.

Here are a few tips based loosely on Garr Reynolds' thinking in his book *Presentation Zen: Simple Ideas on Presentation Design and Delivery* (Reynolds, 2008):

1 **Think as a beginner.** Garr Reynolds calls this 'the mind of a child'. Children are capable of coming up with the most surprising ideas, because they are not weighed down with an adult's mental baggage. So, do the same as a child: look at a subject as though you know nothing about it. Only then will it be possible for fresh, new ideas to spring into your mind.

2   **Think 'out of the box'.** Agreed, it is difficult to have a child-like view of a subject if you are an expert. But experts need to have other qualities besides their expertise. They must be able to free themselves from their paradigm, break fixed habits and escape from closed structures.

3   **Be prepared to make mistakes.** Fear is the greatest enemy of creativity. It limits your vision. Often the best solutions are found only after mistakes have been made. Once you accept this, your creativity will come more easily.

4   **Steal with your eyes.** You don't need to reinvent the wheel. Be prepared to copy. Watch other presentations, adverts, newspaper headlines, magazine covers, etc. Be inspired by others.

5   **Go out.** Don't wait until inspiration hits you like a bolt of lightning in the office – because it could be a long wait! Creative ideas often come at the moments you least expect them: whilst you are out jogging, visiting a museum, or cooking Sunday lunch.

6   **Choose the right moment.** Creativity has its 'right moment'. Some people get their best insights when they are lying in bed at night. Discover your own 'right moment'. Always keep a notepad or smartphone handy, so that you can jot down those brilliant ideas when they strike.

7   **Be enthusiastic.** Really get into your subject. Live, breathe and eat it. Keep it at the forefront of your mind. In this way, your brain will give it priority when it comes to generating new ideas.

8   **Make the most of limitations.** Don't let limitations get you down; use them to make you fly! All revolutionary ideas have their origin in overcoming some limitation. You are allowed to use only five slides? Why not try to say what you have to say in three? Or just one. Or five, each with a single word.

Creative thinking exercise

To shake up those creative brain cells, you might like to try the following two exercises in creative thinking.

Out of the box

Join all the points with four straight lines, without lifting your pen or pencil from the paper. It's not easy, but you can do it, if you think out of the box!

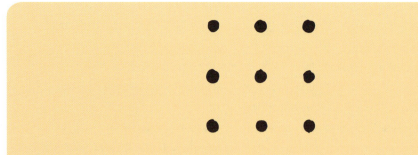

But can you do it with just three straight lines?

Live with your limitations

Nine-year-old Joey solved this problem in a few minutes. Can you be as creative?

A lamp is hanging in an empty room with just a single door. If you leave the room, the door closes, so that no light can penetrate or escape. On the wall outside the room there are three switches. One of them turns on the light. When you are standing by the switches, it is impossible to look into the room. You are allowed to enter the room just once. How can you find out which switch works the light?

(For solutions see **www.edgruwez.com.**)

Two ways to better presentations

As I outlined above, the two main root causes of bad presentations can be summarised as follows:

1 Presentations are inherently difficult to make, because of the curse of knowledge.

2 Most presenters are very badly prepared, because there are too many things to think about and not enough time.

In this book I propose two solutions to overcome these problems:

1 **Make sure that you understand how your audience thinks.** Understand how the cognitive processes work in your audience's mind. It will help you to overcome the curse of knowledge.

2 **Use a process to design your presentation.** In this book I propose the TLSM method to design presentations. By following this method, you will overcome the problem of forgetting important aspects. You will work on the right aspect of your presentation at the right moment. In this way you avoid rework and will produce better presentations in less time.

The next two chapters will give you an introduction to both solutions. Part II of the book describes the TLSM method in full detail.

SOLUTION 1
Understand how your audience thinks

Around the turn of the century I organised a three-day conference for Volvo truck dealers from around Europe. It was an important event in which we shared the company's new strategy and the dealers' role in it. We gathered the dealers in a fantastic remote location on the Swedish coast. Different speakers presented different aspects of the new vision and the strategy.

The start of the conference wasn't easy. The dealers were reluctant. They didn't understand, or so they said. A euphemism for 'I don't agree', I thought. Until, in the afternoon, the SVP of the European Division, Nils, who couldn't be there earlier, gave a 20-minute presentation. Three minutes into his speech the atmosphere in the room changed. Everyone paid attention to every word he said. And, to my big surprise, the audience's earlier confusion entirely disappeared. I still remember the dealers walking out of the room with a smile, saying: 'Now I understand'. Not only did they understand, but they all agreed. And, at a subsequent event, in a discussion with some of those dealers, I noticed that people even remembered exact words from his speech – months later.

I've been thinking a lot about that presentation. The strange thing is that Nils didn't say anything that others hadn't said before him that same day. Yet, when he said it, suddenly everyone understood and agreed. Why was that?

Wouldn't it be interesting to be able to get into people's heads and understand how they think? How do they pay attention? What makes them understand? How can you make someone agree? And how do you make your story stick in their minds for months, and even years?

It's a gift that some people seem to be born with. But you can certainly learn a great deal. Understanding the principles of the 'working memory' and the principles of persuasion, probably will help you more than any list of tips and tricks. So, let me give you a short introduction to the theory of the working memory. Throughout the book I will give further insights into how to use this knowledge to gain attention, make people understand, make them agree and make them remember.

The theory of the working memory: history

The term 'working memory' was coined first in the 1950s by George A. Miller. His work was continued by his colleagues Richard Atkinson and Richard Shiffrin. Alan Baddeley and Graham Hitch, two British psychologists, refined the model further still until the beginning of this century. This is the model on which this book is based. The theory of the working memory is accepted widely as an excellent explanation of how the mechanisms of the human mind deal with communication. Many authors, including Richard Mayer in *Multimedia Learning* and John Medina in *Brain Rules* (two books that I strongly recommend), use the theory to unlock the secrets of the way our brain functions and how people interact with each other (Miller, 1956; Atkinson & Shiffrin, 1968; Baddeley, 1992, 2000; Baddeley & Hitch, 1994; Repovs & Baddeley, 2006; Medina, 2008; Mayer, 2009). The theory has, of course, some limitations, too (see **www.edgruwez.com**).

THE TRINITY OF THE MEMORY

The theory of the working memory distinguishes three different parts to our cognitive brain: the sensory memory, the working memory and the long-term memory.

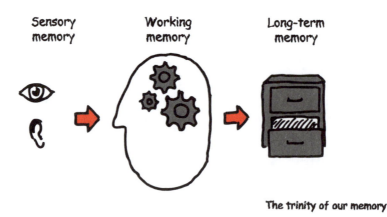

Sensory memory   Working memory   Long-term memory

The trinity of our memory

The sensory memory

The sensory memory is an ultra-short memory that retains visual and auditory signals for a very short period. You can test this easily for yourself. Take a look at the following figure. Close both eyes and open them again. Do this a number of times. You will probably notice that the image remains briefly on your retina, even when your eyes are closed.

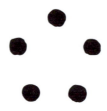

Also, sound is retained briefly in the sensory memory in much the same way. Thousands of different sensory inputs are bombarding your eyes and ears continuously, and all this mass of information is retained for a fraction of a second, two seconds at most. This part of our brain 'sees' the things, but without 'understanding' what they are. That's done in the working memory.

The working memory

This working memory is the centre of your cognitive competencies and the hub for all the information received by the brain. It selects which of the sensory stimuli are worth further consideration and action. This is the part of the brain that focuses your attention, transforms impulses into information, makes decisions and generates new knowledge.

Imagine that you are driving your car. You are listening to the music on the radio, whilst your thoughts are going through the different things you want to do later that day. Your eyes look out of the windscreen and you see many things passing by. None of them gets your particular attention, until your eye catches a large unexpected object in the middle of the road.

The left side of your working memory, the recognising memory, steers your attention and interprets what you see or hear. It will focus your attention immediately on the unexpected object. It will compare the object with other things stored in your long-term memory and recognise it as a concrete mixer that probably fell off a lorry. It passes that information on to the executive memory.

The executive memory is the core of our cognitive brain. It takes decisions and creates new knowledge. It does so by combining the new information with knowledge already stored in your long-term memory: a concrete mixer is made of steel, steel is heavy and hitting heavy things is dangerous, so it decides that it is safer not to hit the object. The knowledge from earlier braking experiences tells us there is not enough distance to stop safely, so it looks at which side you can best avoid the obstacle. It takes that decision in a split second and passes on the necessary signals to your motoric system to set the necessary events in motion.

It also stores the information in your long-term memory, so that you learn from the experience. It is the third time you have had to avoid an object on this road, so maybe in the future you need to be more careful on that road. And in the shorter run, a minute or two after the near collision, the memory of that concrete mixer on the road will set off the thought process that you probably ought to call the police to mention the dangerous obstacle.

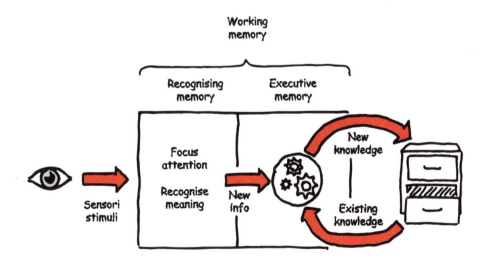

The working memory fully deserves its name. It does a huge amount of work inside the brain. It interprets and combines information to create new knowledge at lightning speed.

Not that the working memory is without its shortcomings. Whereas the sensory memory has an almost unlimited capacity, the working memory has an extremely limited capacity. When you saw the concrete mixer on the road, you certainly didn't read the advertisement on the billboard on the side of the road. And, as soon as you recognised the object as a concrete mixer, all your thoughts about planning your day stopped immediately.

The long-term memory

The long-term memory is the storage place for all our knowledge. This mental 'filing cabinet' can retain huge amounts of information for relatively long periods and is not subject to the same capacity restrictions as the working memory. It remembers what a concrete mixer looks like, knows it is made of steel, and knows that steel is heavy; it knows the braking distance of your car; etc. ... It stores information for years (this is a dangerous road) or for minutes (I should call the police), depending on the nature of the information and the circumstances.

THREE MISCONCEPTIONS

The working of our brain teaches us many things that can be applied usefully in communication and presentations. Throughout the book you will learn how to put a few concrete mixers in your presentation. But first let me point out three of the most important lessons, which counteract three frequent misconceptions.

Dual channel approach

Misconception 1: All information has to be on the slides

- Wrong! The recognising memory consists of a visual and an auditory channel. Treat them as two separate channels that need to be attuned to each other, not copies of each other.

In many presentations people forget that speaking and seeing are two completely different things that co-exist alongside each other. You can explain something just by talking about it, but you can increase your impact when you also show images that illustrate what you are saying. Seeing and hearing are two separate parts of the recognising memory.

Each of these parts has only a limited bandwidth. But, just like you can watch where you are driving whilst listening to the car radio, you can double the total available bandwidth by using both channels alongside each other. This is something that you can – and should – exploit in your presentations. Transmit different, but related, information to your audience along both channels. Just like the sound and image in a film. And, like in a film, the sound and the image must be synchronised perfectly.

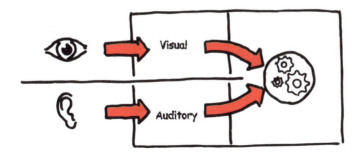

The working memory has dual channels

So, remember to show something on a slide only when you are actually talking about the same subject.

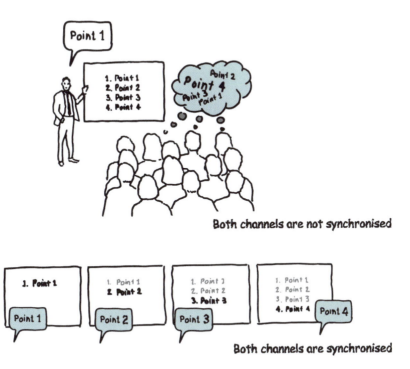

Both channels are not synchronised

Both channels are synchronised

Although, in most cases, both channels work independently of each other, there is one important exception. For reading text, we need to use both the visual and the auditory channel. This is because our ability to understand language is located in the auditory channel. The visual channel recognises the letters and words, but it is the auditory channel that transforms language into meaning.

In other words, we cannot listen to a speaker and read a text simultaneously, unless the speaker is reading out the text in question. For this reason, large amounts of text on slides is a major no-no, and should be avoided at all costs.

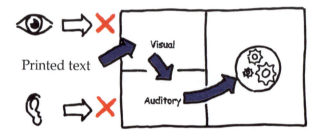

Printed text monopolises both channels

Limited capacity

Misconception 2: The more information, the better

- The capacity of the working memory actually is extremely limited. If the attention of the working memory is focused on unnecessary information, or even decorative elements on your slide, it will have no room to store the things you really want it to store.

The working memory capacity is the number of items that can be processed and stored during a complex memory task (Barrett et al. 2004). Everyone knows that the cognitive capabilities of people are limited. But most of us have no idea just how limited. As early as 1956 the cognitive scientist George Miller carried out his famous 'magic number 7' experiment (Miller, 1956). The exact number is still a subject of discussion, but the general principle of limitation is accepted universally and the number is low. Very, very low. Recent research indicates that it might be as low as three to five (unrelated) pieces of information (Cowan, 2000; Cowan et al. 2004).

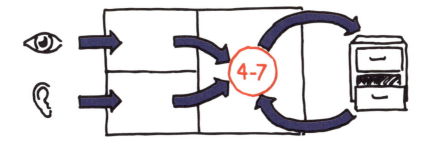

The working memory has a very limited capacity

Many presenters offer their audience too many pieces of information at once. The amount of information that we fire off at the working memory is known as 'the cognitive load'. If there are 10 different things on a single slide, this means that the cognitive load is high. Too high for the audience to absorb it immediately. As a result, people might remember one or two of the less important things or even nothing at all. So, a higher cognitive load means that your listeners will remember less than when the load is set at lower levels. Moreover, cognitive load increases not only with information, but with every input. Even decorative elements will increase the cognitive load for our brain.

Look at the posters in the following diagram. Which of the two can you read most quickly? The first, of course, because it is the simplest. Its cognitive load is lower, since there is less visual information to process. So the first poster leaves more of your cognitive capacity free to actually assimilate the meaning of the message.

Lower cognitive load

Higher cognitive load

By now the moral should be clear: design your story and your slides as simply as possible. Do not give people too many ideas all at once. Scrap everything from your slides that is not essential for your presentation.

The processing of information

Misconception 3: The listener hears and remembers what I say

- In reality, what you say and show does not stick automatically in the audience's minds. They are not human tape recorders! People see, hear and remember things differently.

The working memory interprets, reorganises and changes the information it receives. Because it is so limited in its capacity, the working memory can use only a small amount of the incoming information. So, in order to decide what deserves attention, it constantly compares the incoming information stream with knowledge already stored in the long-term memory. And new knowledge is formed by combining the incoming information with existing knowledge and emotions.

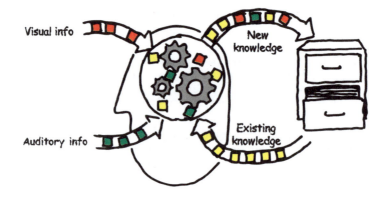

The working memory leaves no input unchanged

But the knowledge stored in the long-term memory is different for everyone in your audience. So, whatever you say and show, the people in the audience will see it and hear it in different ways. And these differences often are much greater than we imagine.

But, if our working memories can handle only a few pieces of information at any one moment, how are we able to build up complex reasoning and acquire complex insights? The answer is that, in the course of its many eons of evolution, the brain has developed strategies to get around this problem: grouping, abstraction and pyramid thinking.

- **Grouping and abstraction.** Because our working memory can deal with a maximum of only four to seven things at any one time, the brain has adopted a strategy to collect similar pieces of information into a group. If you think of what you want to do later today, you don't think in terms of: 'select something to eat tonight, ask the kids if that's okay, look up the recipe, make a shopping list, take the car keys, go out, lock the door …'. You will group all these things and give it a more abstract meaning or a name, like 'shop for supper', which reflects the totality of all you have to do. This abstraction is the summary of the elements in the group: a generic name or the conclusion of all underlying elements. In this way you can think of more complex processes of reasoning: 'Today I want to finish work, pick up the kids, shop for supper and call my mum.' You use the more limited number of abstractions, rather than the individual group elements.

- **Pyramid thinking** means that the brain, in a further step, can also group and summarise these abstract ideas, thereby taking the abstraction process to a higher level. This can be done in different layers, allowing us to develop highly complex reasoning based on many insights, ideas and steps, whilst at the same time requiring the working memory to deal with only four to seven separate things at any moment. Together, these different levels of abstraction form a kind of pyramid. Hence the term 'pyramid thinking'.

Imagine that you are asked to summarise all the makes of car you know. How would you go about it? Perhaps you would group them according to country of origin.

CARS			
FRENCH CARS	**GERMAN CARS**	**JAPANESE CARS**	**ITALIAN CARS**
Renault	BMW	Nissan	Fiat
Citroën	Audi	Toyota	Alfa Romeo
Peugeot	Volkswagen	Honda	Lancia
	Mercedes	Mazda	Ferrari
		Mitsubishi	Maserati
		Subaru	Lamborghini

By understanding this pyramid thinking in detail, we can present information in such a way that it is easy for the working memory to understand. We will be returning to this in more detail in Step 5 of the TLSM method.

The impact of emotions

Various psychological experiments have shown that emotions are capable of influencing our perception of reality. Of course, this is something we all already know: the glass is either half empty or half full, depending on your mood.

When a memory or pattern is anchored in your long-term memory, the emotion that was active at the moment of encoding is stored with it. This means that, when you call up that particular pattern, you also call up its related emotion and vice-versa.

Imagine that you were in Rome on holiday and it rained the whole time, your hotel was lousy and your seafood pizza made you sick. Your memories of this holiday will not be happy ones. So, whenever someone mentions Rome in conversation, your mood darkens. But, if your holiday was fantastic – sunshine every day and you met the person who later became your partner for life – the mention of Rome would brighten your day.

Every memory contains a stored emotional experience. And the stronger this emotional experience was, the more powerful the memory becomes. What are your strongest memories? The birth of your child; the moment you met your partner; how you forgot your text during the school play in front of all the parents; the Christmas tree in your parents' house with all the presents …; All of them have strong emotions linked to them. This has obvious implications for presentations: the stronger the emotional commitment of your audience, the more likely your information will be anchored in their memory.

Emotions make your presentation memorable

Emotions also steer our attention. When we see something that induces fear, for example, it gets our full attention. This is well known by police researchers. When a gun is involved in a crime, the witnesses are less likely to remember the face of the criminal or the colour of the car, because all of their attention goes on the gun.

To summarise, we can say that emotions:

- are stored in our brain along with memories;
- influence which stimuli will get attention;
- play a role in decision-making processes; and
- strengthen our memories, so that we remember them for longer.

These are four very good reasons for working emotions into your presentation.

SOLUTION 2

Use a design process

Once you have read a couple of books about presentations, you will know that there are hundreds of different tips and tricks. In fact, there are so many that it is impossible to remember them all. Impossible, that is, unless you have a method that allows you to classify them. This is exactly what a design process does. It brings order to the chaos. It is a logical, step-by-step plan that will lead you to better results – time after time.

I have put all relevant tips and recent insights together into one process and called it the TLSM method. The TLSM method is based partly on the insights of Richard Mayer. In his excellent book *Multimedia Learning*, he offers 12 scientifically based principles for multimedia presentations (Mayer, 2009). Although Mayer's principles were developed for the learning process in an academic environment, they are very useful for developing better presentations and slides. For this reason, I have integrated his principles into my approach and supplemented them to arrive at a total of 25 insights or rules for good presentations (**www.edgruwez.com**).

The design process of the TLSM method was developed empirically, supported by scientific insights. It evolved further with the input of the many presentation designers who have applied the method to the process. This modification continued right up to the moment when I decided to put pen to paper for this book. But even this is not the end. The methodology will continue to evolve, of that I am sure.

Not everything in the TLSM method is unique. In Part II you will, doubtless, read things that you have already read or heard before. What is unique is the integration of all these different insights into a clear process and the division of that process into four separate phases.

FOUR PHASES

The Greek philosopher Aristotle was praised universally for his teaching of rhetoric. Even though he wrote his insights many centuries ago, they are still valuable, even today. Aristotle distinguished three elements that need to be present in order to convince an audience:

- ethos or ethical appeal: invoke trustworthiness;
- logos or logical appeal: convince by use of reason and logic;
- pathos or emotional appeal: invoke sympathy.

These three elements are nothing less than the first three phases in the design process of the TLSM method:

- ethos: the **T**hinking;
- logos: the **L**ogic;
- pathos: the **S**tory; and
- the fourth: the **M**edia.

(We can hardly blame Aristotle for forgetting to consider the role of PowerPoint!)

Thinking, Logic, Story, Media are the phases of the TLSM design method. In other words, whenever you are preparing a presentation, you need to run through these four phases, one after the other. And you have to do so in precisely that order. Many people make the mistake of trying to do all four things at once, so that they become horribly confused. And so does their audience.

The end result of your presentation must, of course, match your original intention. For this reason, I have visualised the process as a circle.

Phase 1 The Thinking	Take a step back and look at the bigger picture. Find somewhere quiet and take time to think about the essence of your presentation. Why should they listen to you? What do you want to achieve? How are you going to achieve it?
Phase 2 The Logic	You first need to fix the objective content of your presentation. Think logically. What are you going to talk about? More importantly, what are you not going to talk about? What is the key of your argument? Are all your ideas logically connected? How can you structure these ideas so that they can be understood easily?
Phase 3 The Story	When you have fixed the objective content of your presentation, you can start to write your story. This requires a more creative approach. You must find ways to make your story appealing and memorable.
Phase 4 The Media	In this final phase you now need to find the best way to implement it. This involves making slides and preparing documents that support your key message. Double-check everything to make sure that it all goes smoothly on the day. If you have done the previous three phases properly, this should be a piece of cake.

Each phase in the TLSM method consists of 3 steps, adding up to 12 steps in total.

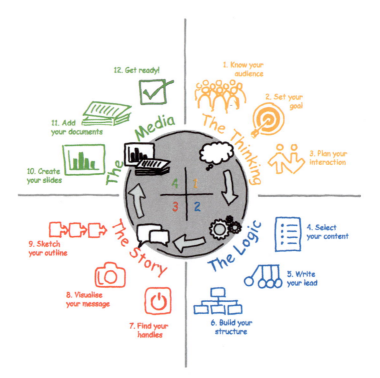

Phase 1 The Thinking	
Step 1: Know your audience	Why should they listen to you?
Step 2: Set your goal	What do you want to achieve?
Step 3: Plan your interaction	How are you going to achieve it?
Phase 2 The Logic	
Step 4: Select the content	What are you going to talk about; and what not?
Step 5: Write your lead	Find an introduction that will pull your audience into the presentation.
Step 6: Build your structure	Structure your ideas so that they can be understood easily.
Phase 3 The Story	
Step 7: Find your handles	Add emotion, story and sensory detail to your ideas.
Step 8: Visualise your message	Find images that will stick in their minds.
Step 9: Sketch your outline	Bring it all together into a slick story.
Phase 4 The Media	
Step 10: Create your slides	Make your (PowerPoint) slides.
Step 11: Add your documents	Add reader documents and speaker notes.
Step 12: Get ready!	Make sure everything is ready for your presentation.

DESIGNING IN FOUR MINDSETS

One of the philosophies behind the four phases is that you work more efficiently when you adopt a different mindset for each phase.

1 **The Thinking:** requires a helicopter view, viewing things from a distance, seeing the bigger picture and thinking in terms of metaphors.

2 **The Logic:** requires a business-like, analytical mindset, thinking in critical, logical and factual terms.

3 **The Story:** requires a human, emotional and creative mindset, asking how you can involve, convince and touch the hearts of your audience.

4 **The Media:** requires a practical, implementing mindset, adding the fine detail and efficiently putting the messages in words, on slides and on paper.

By using four different mindsets for the four different phases you will perform much better than when you try to do everything at once. A creative mindset is sometimes difficult to reconcile with logic and a logical mindset often will stifle your creativity. The different mindsets also will help you to use your time more efficiently. For example, once you begin with your slides it is better not to allow your creativity to distract you from the task at hand. It is also counterproductive at this stage to allow your logic to change the structure of the presentation. This must be fixed before you start the slides – otherwise you can keep on going round in circles.

DESIGN IS THINKING BACKWARDS

The four phases are also linked to the functioning of the working memory. This, too, has four distinct steps (although this is a simplification of a much more complex reality).

- **Step 1:** the sensory memory receives signals from the senses, so that we see and hear. These signals are stored only for a very short time.
- **Step 2:** the recognising memory chooses some of these stimuli. These are given attention and are interpreted. This is a very subjective process, during which the recognising memory uses emotions and compares the stimuli with existing patterns in the long-term memory.
- **Step 3:** the executive memory organises the incoming information into a coherent structure. In this way, it creates new knowledge. In the context of your presentation this is a conscious, objective and conceptualising process.
- **Step 4:** the long-term memory stores this new knowledge.

The 'four-phase design method' approaches these four steps in the reverse order:

- **Phase 1:** design for the long-term memory. Define what information you want to be stored by the long-term memories of your listeners. First you need to know what they already know and feel. Then you can decide how you want to change that.
- **Phase 2:** design for the executive memory. Define the concepts and ideas that will change those long-term memories. Give them a coherent pyramidal structure, so that the executive memory will understand clearly. Make it logical, so that everything fits together.
- **Phase 3:** design for the recognising memory. Colour your messages with emotions, stories and sensory information. To ensure that the executive memory gets the right input, you need to focus attention on the right information, which must then be interpreted in the right way. You can do this by using the right subjective and/or emotional content. This content must attract and feed attention.
- **Phase 4:** design for the sensory memory. Design the slides, words and documents that will be picked up by your audience's sensory memory.

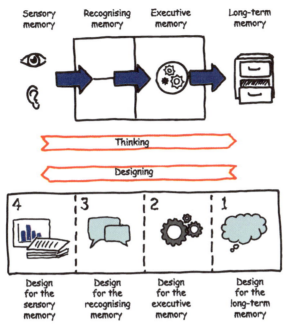

Sensory memory   Recognising memory   Executive memory   Long-term memory

Thinking

Designing

4   3   2   1

Design for the sensory memory   Design for the recognising memory   Design for the executive memory   Design for the long-term memory

Designing is thinking backwards

ARE THE FOUR PHASES REALLY NECESSARY?

Four phases, and twelve steps, just to make a single presentation? It seems like a lot. Is it all really necessary? Some people, no doubt, will complain that they don't have the time. Sometimes there just isn't enough time. When this happens, it is tempting to skip straight to phase 4, immediately drawing up your slides without any prior preparation. But, believe me, inevitably this will lead to bad presentations and even greater loss of time.

Winston Churchill once said: 'I'm going to make a long speech because I've not had the time to prepare a short one.' Making a concise presentation takes time. But the four-phase approach will help you to keep this time to a minimum.

Some of the steps take only a couple of minutes. Even so, it is important that you get yourself into the right mindset for every phase and reflect on each individual step. The minutes that you invest in these activities will be more than recouped when you come to make your slides and you are actually standing in front of your audience.

But is it not possible to make it all a bit shorter? Here the old adage applies: 'First learn the rules before you break them.'

I am not pretending that my method is the only answer to your presentation problems. But the method has at least proven itself to be effective in practice. Many people reported that it reduced their preparation time by 30 per cent. This does not mean that it has to be used like a straightjacket! I like to think of it in terms of the philosophy of the Oriental martial arts, where the pupil needs to pass through three phases of development:

- **First: obedience.** Do exactly what the teacher tells you.
- **Second: practice.** Apply what the teacher taught you, in the way that he taught you.
- **Third: improvise.** Only when you master all the basic movements will it be possible for you to adjust their use to reflect different circumstances and your own style.

Presentation training

So, to begin with, it is a good idea to follow the method in full. When you have gained experience, you might be able to cut corners, but only if you remember the following advice:

1 Stick to the basic philosophy; always follow the spirit of the method.

2 Always keep the four phases of the design process separate and implement them in the right order: first things first!

3 Remember that the phases decline successively in importance. In other words, the first phase is more important than the last. If your slides aren't 100 per cent perfect, this is less crucial than if you haven't got a clue about the purpose and objective of your presentation.

Of one thing you can be sure: when you have mastered the TLSM method, you will begin your next presentation with much more confidence than ever before.

HOW DO YOU ALLOCATE YOUR TIME?

What percentage of time should be spent on each phase? Based on my observations of hundreds of presenters, the allocation of time before using the TLSM method is roughly as follows:

- 1–3 per cent of time is spent on thinking about the objective, the audience and the message.
- 4–12 per cent is spent on gathering and structuring the content.
- 85–95 per cent is spent on designing and amending slides and handouts.

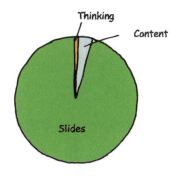

How managers spend their preparation time

You don't need to be Einstein to see that this allocation is woefully out of balance. The bulk of the time is devoted to the design of the powerpoint, with almost no time being devoted to the essential preparatory brainwork. When I ask my trainees why this is, usually they answer: 'I know what I want to say.' And so they begin to design their slides immediately. But this is not the way it works. Once you are busy designing your slides, this demands your full attention and so the crucial questions often remain unanswered. Inevitably this leads to bad presentations.

The TLSM method proposes the following very different allocation of time:

How managers should spend their preparation time

- The Thinking = 5–20 per cent.
- The Logic = 30–40 per cent.
- The Story = 15–25 per cent.
- The Media = 30–40 per cent.

PART II

BUILDING *your* PRESENTATION

PHASE 1
THE THINKING

What is your presentation for?

AUDIENCE – GOAL – INTERACTION

I recently heard a marketing director speaking to one of her managers: 'David, I have just heard that I need to give a presentation to the executive management team at nine o'clock tomorrow morning. They want to know how far we have got with the project. Can you make me some slides by tomorrow morning? If I have them in time for the meeting, that'll be fine. I'll just talk through your slides.'

Does this sound familiar? I bet it does. What struck me most about her reaction was that final comment: 'I'll talk through your slides'. I could almost see her presentation unfolding before me. There she stands, talking to her slides instead of her audience ...

Kate – that was her name – didn't seem to think it was necessary to test the water with her audience in advance. She didn't know her slides, and so she would just read off what they said. In other words, she couldn't adjust her content to reflect what she saw on the faces of the executive management team.

She was convinced that this 'casual' approach – without any preparation – would work. But things turned out very differently from what she expected! What she didn't know was that the CFO wanted to make cuts in the budget. She also didn't know that a project proposed by the HR director had been turned down recently for the same budget reasons. Now he was determined to show that these money-guzzling marketing projects were a pure waste of money compared with his 'vital' HR project.

You can guess the rest. Kate walked straight into an ambush and her project was cancelled. But it was really her own fault, because she was badly prepared. She had made no effort to put herself in the position of her listeners and she paid the price. Because this is where the preparation must begin: with your audience.

'Think before you speak.' Do not underestimate the importance of this simple advice. In fact, it is more than just 'important'. It is the most important thing of all.

You often think you know your audience. After all, you know who you are presenting to, don't you? A customer, a project group, the executive management team ... But are these people for or against your plans? Are they optimistic or pessimistic? Do they have enough background information to understand what you want to say? What kind of arguments will most appeal to them? What are they expecting from you? When I ask these questions during my training sessions, I am surprised still by the lack of answers I receive. The majority of the trainees think they know their audience, but this 'knowledge' is based often on little more than assumptions.

The same is true for the objectives of the presentation. People say that they know what they want to achieve and, if you ask them to put that objective into words, the answer usually is vague and inconclusive. But, if they themselves hardly know where they are going, how can they expect their audience to follow them?

And then out come the classic excuses: from 'I don't have time for that' to the self-assured 'I know what my objective is, so I don't have to think about it'. After you have read the next few pages, you will probably think differently.

The start of everything: Why?

In 2009 Simon Sinek, an ex-advertising man and now a full-time consultant and speaker (on TED, amongst other things), wrote the fascinating book *Start with Why* (Sinek, 2009). He explains how great leaders are able to inspire others to action. The key question, according to Sinek, is: 'Why?'. If you ask yourself the why question, you will already be moving a long way in the right direction. And until you have a clear and final answer to this why question, you are not ready to make your presentation.

So always start with the why question:

- Why is your presentation necessary? Why should anyone bother to listen to it?

This will lead on to other questions:

- About your audience: who are these people?
- About your objective: what do you want to achieve?
- About the setting: how are you going to achieve it?

Alonetime

We are always very busy, so we seldom have time to take a step back and look at our work. But, if you are dealing with something important like a presentation, you need to take a little extra time to think seriously about the really essential questions. Or, as Garr Reynolds puts it in his book *Presentation Zen*: 'Slow down to see' (Reynolds, 2008).

What's more, it is important that you should not spend this thinking time stuck behind your own desk. To think clearly, you must be able to free yourself from your normal working environment. So go for a walk or a bike ride. Have a coffee in the café down the road. Change your rhythm, so that time can stand still. You will be amazed how much more clearly you can see things.

The research carried out by psychologist Ester Buchholz proved the value of 'alonetime' (Buchholz, 1998). Being alone is an absolute necessity for our brain if we want to combine ideas, reach higher levels of abstraction and see the things that are truly essential. Buchholz expresses it as follows:

'Life's creative solutions require alonetime. Solitude is required for the unconscious to process and unravel problems. Others inspire us, information feeds us, practice improves our performance, but we need quiet time to figure things out, to emerge with new discoveries, to unearth original answers.'

STEP 1
Know your audience
Why should they listen to you?

I can still remember my first day in the second year of primary school. We had a teacher called Mr De Wilde. Of all the teachers I have had in my time, he was the strictest – by miles! That morning, Mr De Wilde caught me talking to my desk-mate in class. He gave us both a dressing-down that made our hair stand on end. There was one sentence from his diatribe that has always stayed with me: 'Gruwez, do you know why a human being has two ears and just one mouth?' The question didn't need an answer. Years later I discovered that Mr De Wilde had borrowed the words from the Greek philosopher Epictetus: 'We have two ears and just one mouth so that we can listen twice as much as we speak.'

This quotation contains a deeper truth: the first thing you must do is listen. If you don't know your audience, you cannot know what will convince them or appeal to them, and your presentation will achieve little. So start by developing a sense of what your audience feels. What interests them and what moves them?

Most people who have to speak in front of an audience experience a degree of stress. They feel uncertain and are concerned about the possible reactions. They are worried that they will forget their text. As a result, they focus too much on themselves and lose sight of the most important thing: their audience.

Your focus on your audience is more important than your slides, more crucial than your style of delivery and even more essential than your message. You need to assess constantly whether what you are saying will be relevant and meaningful for them or not. Even during the presentation, look for their reactions, try to sense their emotions – and adjust your presentation accordingly. It is the only way to truly reach them. But, before you can 'play' your audience in this manner, it is first necessary to do your homework. In fact, this is where you must always start.

Remember Simon Sinek and his book *Start with Why*: why should your audience listen to you? What do you have to say that they will want to hear? Finding the answers to these questions won't happen all by itself. It takes time and effort.

FIRST UNDERSTAND AND THEN YOU WILL BE UNDERSTOOD

Stephen Covey is a well-known name in management circles. He wrote the bestseller *The 7 Habits of Highly Effective People.* One of these seven habits is: 'Seek first to understand, then be understood' (Covey, 2004). Covey calls this empathic listening and it is one of the qualities found in all good leaders.

But what is empathic listening? Above all, it means listening with the intention of really understanding the other person. This may sound obvious, but it isn't. Most of us hear the words, but don't stop to think what they actually mean. Active listening requires effort: you need to immerse yourself in the reference frames of your conversation partner; see the world through their eyes; explore their paradigms and sense their emotions. Empathic listening means understanding the other person both intellectually and emotionally. This is something that you can use to your advantage in your presentations.

What's more, it also increases their willingness to listen to you. You can compare it with being a doctor. First he needs to listen to the patient before he can make a proper diagnosis. How would you feel if you walked into his consulting room and he immediately started telling you what was wrong with you, before you even had a chance to sit down? Well, that's how a presentation audience feels if you don't listen to them.

SEE THE INDIVIDUAL IN THE GROUP

Ask a colleague who is about to give a presentation if he knows who his audience are. In 90 per cent of cases the answer will be: 'Of course I know – it's the management team!' (or the sales staff, the HR team or the line managers, etc.). But these are boxes in an organigram, they aren't real people. You are not making your presentation to a group, but to the individuals who make up that group. To Karen, Barbara, Peter, Vince, Andy and Julie. Each of them has their own preferences and style – and it is your task to find out what they are.

If you do no more than regard your audience as an anonymous group, your presentation will be equally anonymous. It will be very difficult to make genuine contact with your audience. You become like a radio, playing background 'muzak' to which no one is really listening.

It is much better to try and give your listeners a face. Look at them as individuals. Karen, aged 40, ambitious, mother of three, the sporty type. Wary of new situations, cautious and sensitive about her status in the company. This is a good pen-picture that you can use to set the right tone in your presentation. Of course, I can hear you all saying that it is impossible to take account of every individual in the audience. Kate is like this, but Barbara and Peter are like that. And as for Vince! This is a fair criticism. But there is nothing to stop you picking out the person who is most representative. Or the person who has most influence. Or the person who will be taking the final decision. Focus on key figures, but without making the others feel excluded.

Persona

But what if you are making a presentation to a large audience? Is it possible to see them as anything other than an amorphous mass? Yes, it is. Try to visualise a few typical people from the audience. Create two or three fictive characters in your head. See them as real individuals. Try to form a mental picture of who they are, what they do, how they think. Hold these imaginary people at the forefront of your mind during the preparation of your presentation. It will make your task easier and the end result more direct and more personal.

The designers of services and user interfaces also use this technique. They refer to these imaginary people as 'persona'. They are detailed descriptions of non-existent beings, who are typical of someone in the target group for which they are designing.

By describing these persona in detail, they get a clear image of who they are (or could be, if they existed). This allows the designers to do their work in a more human-focused way. They are not designing abstractly, but are designing for: 'Rachel, aged 38, married, well-educated, likes a good glass of wine, is mad about sushi and still visits her parents each weekend ...' Add a photo to this description and you have created a perfect persona.

REALLY GET TO KNOW THE PEOPLE

Annette Simmons, author of *Whoever Tells the Best Story Wins*, talks about conducting a real 'body search' when she refers to learning about your audience (Simmons, 2007). Interact with them. Talk to them. Call them. Ask questions. Look at their LinkedIn profiles or their Facebook pages. Google their names; you will be amazed what you can find.

Make use of this information. Is one of the key figures in your audience a marathon runner? If so, compare the difficult task you are discussing with running a marathon. Does he play golf? Compare the three steps in fine-tuning your cost estimate with driving, chipping and putting.

Ambassadors and terrorists

Most presentations deal with the introduction of new ideas or the taking of important decisions. You want to bring about change, and this often provokes resistance. For this reason, it is important to try and gauge in advance how the audience will react to your proposals.

To do this, you need to find out about their current thinking. Are they optimistic or pessimistic? What do they know of your ideas? Are they likely to be for or against?

A good tool is to use an adoption ladder. At which rung on the ladder is your audience currently situated? Your objective is to use your presentation to move them up the ladder. Each rung has its own specific arguments. So it is important to know where you are starting from. The ladder looks like this:

Unaware	Knows nothing about your ideas.
Aware	Is aware of your ideas, without really knowing them.
Understands	Understands the meaning of your ideas.
Supports	Thinks positively about your ideas.
Involved	Actively searches for arguments to support your ideas.
Committed	Influences others to support your ideas.
Ambassador	Does everything possible to successfully realise your ideas.

The first three steps on the adoption ladder are emotionless. The remaining four steps involve increasing levels of emotional commitment. During a presentation it is quasi-impossible to raise someone from the 'unaware' level to the 'ambassador' level. At best, you can hope to get him/her one or two rungs up the ladder. So be realistic and don't aim for too much.

Don't forget that people will be both for and against you. There is also such a thing as a rejection ladder. Your ideas can turn people off emotionally, so that they become your fiercest opponents.

Unaware	Knows nothing about your ideas.
Aware	Knows something about your ideas.
Understands	Thinks he understands your ideas, but doesn't really want to listen.
Resists	Votes against your ideas, when asked.
Opposes	Actively seeks arguments to reject your ideas.
Obstructs	Takes action to defeat your ideas.
Terrorist	Does everything possible to eliminate your ideas.

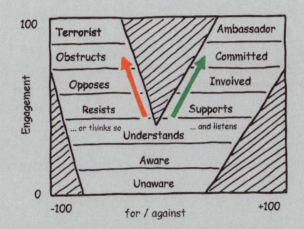

During a presentation usually it will be your intention to move your audience in a positive direction. If you push too hard, you run the risk that they will move towards the left side instead of the right side. And once you have pushed someone into resistance, it is that much harder to get them back. So don't try and turn 'unawares' into 'ambassadors' overnight. This will only create unnecessary opposition. People will move when they are 'ready' – and not before.

USE YOUR SUPPORTERS

One day I was present at a meeting when a CEO addressed his entire staff: '... and these are last year's results: an increase in sales of 3.5 per cent. This is the biggest increase in the market and I am confident that we will soon be bigger than all our competitors put together. Congratulations!' He paused. Two people began to clap. Seconds later, the whole room had joined in. And who were the two brave souls? One was René, the sound and light technician, and the other one was me. Neither of us even worked for the company!

Why shouldn't you ask your supporters to actively support you during your presentation? Nothing too excessive, of course. But a little push in the right direction can't do any harm.

You can ask one of your supporters to express their opinion or give an example: 'It's right what he says, we do need more product training. I was recently at a dealer's who couldn't tell me the difference between the old and the new models.' It goes without saying that these interventions must be sincere and based on the truth. But, if done properly, they can strengthen your credibility and increase your audience's level of involvement greatly. This is a good thing, but don't overdo it.

UNDERSTAND YOUR OPPONENTS

Also, remember to reach out to your opponents. Make yourself familiar with their objections and show understanding for their position, before explaining why their fears are groundless. This could save you from a number of unpleasant reactions. Hardcore opposition is the worst nightmare of anyone who wants to get a proposal approved. So be prepared for resistance; understand it in order to know how you can counter it.

SPEAK THE LANGUAGE OF YOUR AUDIENCE

No two people are alike. We all have our own preferences and habits. This is also true of your audience. It is even true for yourself! There are a number of tools you can use to take account of these differences. One of them is the **Herrmann Brain Dominance Instrument (HBDI)**, which helps you to see differences in personality, so that you can adapt your presentation accordingly.

In short, we all have our own way of thinking. Some of us think analytically, others think in procedures. You might be more creative, whilst I am more emotional-empathic. By mapping the thought preferences of your audience, you can get a better picture of both your audience and yourself. This latter aspect is just as important. If you know that you are an analytical thinker, then you can assume reasonably that you will give your presentations in an analytical manner.

But some of your listeners will be more emotional-empathic. They will find little to enthuse them in your analytical and logical arguments.

Similarly, usually there will be a number of executive staff in your audience, practical-minded people who think in terms of plans, systems and procedures. Once again, your analyses will leave them cold and disinterested. And what about the innovators, who look down on the rest of us from the mountain tops of their creativity? Can you give them the helicopter-view of your ideas that they will expect?

This is one of your biggest challenges: to pitch your presentation in a manner that you are not wholly comfortable with. Can your analytical mind reach out to people who are more creatively, emotionally or practically inclined? Can you put your arguments in their language? And can you do it without losing your own spontaneity?

All the colours of the rainbow

An instrument that can help to personalise your presentation is the Herrmann Brain Dominance Instrument (HBDI) that categorises personal thinking styles in four colours or quadrants (Herrmann, 1996). The model was developed by Ned Herrmann, who for many years was in charge of General Electric's overseas training program. Although I have sound reasons to question its so-called scientific and neurological fundamentals, it has proven to be of practical value in designing communication messages.

Herrmann – a physicist by training – was fascinated by the way the human brain works. He categorised personal differences in four dominant or preferential ways of thinking, which he visualised graphically in four quadrants:

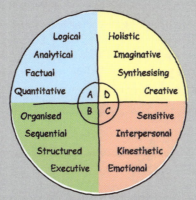

Source: Herrmann, N., The Whole Brain Business Book: Unlocking the power of whole brain thinking in organizations and individuals, © 1996, published by McGraw-Hill Education. Reproduced with permission of McGraw-Hill Education.

Everyone adopts one or more of these four ways of thinking. Some people think logically and analytically. Others are more creatively inclined. A third group prefers to approach things systematically. There is also a group that focuses on emotion.

This means that different lines of argument are appropriate for each thinking method. Imagine that you are trying to introduce a change project in your organisation. Below you will find the typical arguments you could use to convince the four different thinking styles.

	TYPICAL STYLE	TYPICAL MESSAGE
Blue	Business-like, with a logical structure	Stress positive 'return on investment'. Explain the logic and the numbers.
Yellow	Creative, with lots of visual elements	Show how change can contribute to the 'higher goal'. Emphasise originality.
Red	People-centred, interactive	Stress the role of people. What will it mean for them? How will they benefit?
Green	Highly structured, step-by-step approach	Show that all aspects are covered. Stress the flawless implementation plan, which foresees all possible risks.

But don't be too quick to pigeon-hole people in a specific box. We all use the four ways of thinking, but with differing degrees of intensity. One or two colours will be dominant, but all four will be present to some extent. As a speaker, you also have your own dominant style. You must identify this, so that you can take account of other styles during your presentation. If you have a very 'yellow' communication style, you will need to add a little blue, red and green to your discourse. If you don't, you risk losing your audience – because it will certainly contain people with other dominant ways of thinking.

There has been legitimate criticism of this colour model, but in practice it is a simple and useful tool to adjust your communication style to your audience. And, as long as you don't use it as a psychometric tool to categorise or judge people, there is no harm done.

IN SHORT

To begin with, you have done the most important thing: getting to know your audience. You now know who the key figures are. And you know what they know and think about your subject. You have also enlisted supporters to help you and you are ready to show understanding to your opponents.

STEP 2
Set your goal
What do you want to achieve?

I once had the good fortune to attend a board meeting at General Motors. People had flown in from everywhere to put forward their projects. It was the chairman's habit to ask each presenter first to summarise their proposal in a single sentence. One of the senior managers failed hopelessly: 'Well, er, we carried out a study and I would like to show you the results. I've got all the facts and figures here. It might be interesting ...' The chairman interrupted him: 'Cut the crap. What do you want to tell us?' 'Well, the results of the study ...' Another interruption: 'And what do you expect us to do with those results?' 'Er, I don't know really. I just wanted to share them with you.' 'For Christ's sake! If you don't know what you expect of us, what the hell are you doing here? If you don't know what you are going to say, why on earth should we bother to listen? I think you should go back home and think about it. Come back in a month when you have something to tell us.' The poor man had travelled all the way from Germany, and was now sent packing on the next plane home. I can still see the look of embarrassment and disappointment on his face.

Perhaps you think the chairman was unkind, rude, even aggressive? Maybe he was – but he wanted to set an example. And he was right. If you don't have a clear objective or a clear message, why should you waste the time of 20 other people?

This is another crucial point: you must have a clear objective for your presentation. Because it is only when you have an objective that you can actually start thinking about the best way to achieve it.

People often assume that the transmission of knowledge is the objective of a presentation. You know something and want to share it with others. But is that really so? No, there is more to it than that. Knowledge transfer is not an end in itself. It is a means to an end – and that end is change.

When you give a presentation, you always have change in mind. Your audience comes into the room with a certain knowledge, attitude, ability and intention, as registered in their long-term memory. By the time they leave the room after your presentation, you want to have changed them. But what do you want to change? Here are some examples:

- You want to make them aware of the changed circumstances.
- You want to give them new instructions.
- You want to stimulate them, wake them up to the realities of the situation.
- You want to convince them, to get them on your side.
- You want decisions to be taken and problems to be solved.

In other words, you want to change something in their long-term memory. The neural networks in their brain must be altered from what they were before you stood up to speak. They must think differently and act differently. If you don't want to change things, why bother making the presentation in the first place? Even if you need to give an update on a current project where there is really nothing to report, your objective still will be a change: to take away doubt, to reassure people that the project will be completed on time and within budget.

Knowing your objective and formulating it correctly are important for the following reasons:

1 **It sharpens your mind and focuses your work.** You can better organise your arguments if you are working towards an objective.

2 **It helps to define the boundaries of your presentation.** Information that doesn't contribute towards your objective can be jettisoned. This will make your arguments more 'to the point'.

Do you know what your objective is? Write it down immediately in one or two sentences. Is it clear and unambiguous? This is more difficult than it sounds. You instinctively think that you know what your objective is, but your own thoughts are often hazy and imprecise until you get them down on paper. But difficult or not, a clearly defined objective is crucial for the rest of your presentation.

A good objective

- is sufficiently general, but also contains concrete elements;
- is an end in itself, not the way to reach it;
- is ambitious enough to make people enthusiastic;
- must remain valid, even if circumstances change.

Examples of good objectives include:

- 'I want the board to increase my department's budget by x thousand euros.'
- 'The sales team must realise that we need to act quickly if we want to maintain our market position.'
- 'The doctors need to understand the benefits of this new treatment and be willing to test it next month.'
- 'At least 15 per cent of the participants must be willing to sell our products after the presentation.'
- 'The committee must be reassured that my project doesn't get in the way of others.'
- 'The audience must be able to better assess the risks of complex financial products.'

FORMULATE YOUR OBJECTIVE AT THREE LEVELS

Your objective is change, change in the memory programs of your target audience. This change takes place at three different levels: knowing, feeling and doing. **Knowing** is the knowledge that you want to share with the participants. **Feeling** is the emotion of the participants, which will fix your message more prominently and firmly in their minds. **Doing** is the action you wish the participants to take afterwards. All three levels are part of your objective. So let's look at them in a little more detail.

Know

Ask anyone to explain the purpose of their presentation and 99 times out of 100 you will get the answer 'knowledge transfer'! You want to share something with the other person that they currently don't know. But knowledge transfer is more than simply giving people bits of information. The human brain does not work like a kind of 'drop-box', in which you just dump information that is automatically stored. In his book *Multimedia Learning*, Richard Mayer of the University of California calls this the 'empty vessel view' (Mayer, 2009).

If the straightforward provision of information is your only objective, you need to ask yourself whether or not a presentation is the best tool to use. You can transfer information in many other ways, without making people sit and listen to you for half an hour or more. You can use email. Better still, store your information in the cloud or on a server, so that it is available to everyone whenever they need it.

Real knowledge transfer goes beyond the passing of pieces of information from one person to another. It is a complex activity of creating meaning and significance.

Feel

Psychological research has convincingly shown that every decision a person makes – no matter how rational it might seem – is influenced by emotion. We decide something because we **know** that it is the right thing to do:

- **Rational:** 'I **think** that it is right.' You base your decision on information.
- **Emotional:** 'It **feels** right.' You are comfortable with the decision.
- **Combined:** if you **think** it is right and it **feels** right, then you say, 'I **know** it is right' and you can take the decision in full confidence.

In other words, you never decide exclusively on the basis of the facts, but also because you believe in an idea or like a person. Once you realise this, it must be obvious that a presentation also needs a strong emotional component. In fact, many decisions are taken on a purely emotional basis, with the rationalisation coming only afterwards.

The secondary objective of your presentation, therefore, always must be to stimulate sufficient emotional commitment from your audience. This emotional element is so fundamental that it surprises me constantly how little it is mentioned when I ask people to write down their presentation objectives. The reason for this is partly that people seldom think in terms of emotional objectives and partly because emotional objectives are so difficult to describe. But you have to try. The good news is that you will notice quickly how your presentations become more effective once you are able formulate objectives in emotional terms. By naming the emotion, you will display it more easily and pass it on to your audience.

- 'I want the audience to feel **uncomfortable**, because things are not going as they should.'
- 'I want to **reassure** the management that the project is on target.'
- 'I want to make people **curious** about the working of our new product.'
- 'I want to make our sales team **enthusiastic** about our new advertising campaign.'
- 'I want the consumer to **fall in love** with our new range.'
- 'I want our dealers who sell risky products to **lie awake at night**.'

You can think of dozens of emotional objectives of this kind. But be realistic in your expectations. If nobody knew about your product before the presentation, you can't expect it to start selling like hot cakes five minutes after you have sat down. If it is the first time your staff have heard about the new policy, you can't expect them to be wildly enthusiastic straight away. If you can persuade people to move just one rung up the adoption ladder, you can already count this as a success.

Do

The ultimate objective of a presentation in a business context is frequently to bring about concrete action. Something needs to happen, and your presentation is the tool to make sure it does. Consequently, this 'action' element also needs to be included in your objectives. Don't make it too vague: 'I want the team to implement our strategy.' It is much better to be specific: 'I want the team to draw up a 10-point action plan by next Friday that will implement our strategy within three months.'

Typical action objectives include:

- deciding between different alternatives (projects, appointments, etc.);
- implementing a project within a given time frame;
- informing and engaging other people;
- developing ideas within a given time frame;
- drawing up an action plan;
- deciding which products to purchase.

WRITE A POWERFUL KEY MESSAGE

Imagine that a politician is seeking re-election. He is walking through town and suddenly bumps into a TV crew. The reporter pushes a microphone under his nose. The cameras roll. He is live on air! 'What do you have to say to our viewers?' He is given just 10 seconds to come up with a powerful message that will convince the voters – and, if he doesn't do it, he might be looking for a new job after the elections.

It is just the same with presentations: you need to be able to explain your key message in 10 seconds to someone without hesitation and without thinking. So write this key message down at the beginning of your preparation and learn it so thoroughly that it becomes second-nature to you. You need to look at its formulation critically. Don't be satisfied with vague and easy texts like this one:

> 'We tested three concepts for our advertising campaign: the dinosaur concept where we portray ourselves as a friendly dinosaur; the back-to-the-future concept, where we seek to combine the best of the past and the present; and the big-brother concept, where we focus on the welfare of our customers. The dinosaur concept scored best, except in rural areas, where the back-to-the-future concept was the most popular.'

This is not a bad summary, but it is too long. It needs be shorter – and more powerful.

> 'With the dinosaur concept, our campaign will be a success in every town in the country.'

This is positive, concise, sounds good and makes you curious to hear more.

A key message is a single sentence with a single key thought. Long, complex sentences are not really appropriate. The most frequent objection against one-liner key messages is that they don't say enough when there is so much to say. But this is an easy excuse. You just need to keep on looking until you find the right one-liner that says it all. And, to do this, you must make choices. What is the most important thing of all? What is the one thing that your audience must remember above all others?

Many leading companies summarise their strategy in a single sentence; sometimes in just a few words. When Volkswagen refers to itself as *Das Auto*, everyone knows what they mean and what they stand for: German, reliable, the reference, the benchmark. Likewise, if you think of British Airways' 'The world's favourite airline', you think of an airline that can take you absolutely anywhere on the globe with superb quality, friendly service and in top comfort.

And that is how you need to package the proposal in your presentation: short, sweet, but with a real punch.

'If you say three things, you don't say anything.'

James Carvill, campaign leader for Bill Clinton

Tips for a clear key message

1 **Make choices.** It is true that sometimes a presentation will have more than one objective and therefore more than one key message. But there is always one message that is more important than the rest.

2 **Synthesise.** If you can't choose between three key messages, look for a higher level of abstraction that will allow you to combine the three messages into one.

3 **Think about splitting up your presentation.** If you are convinced that you have two equally essential key messages that cannot be combined, you may need to consider giving two separate presentations. You should certainly avoid trying to package too many messages in the same story. Each presentation has its own dynamic and often its own audience.

4 **Search for a metaphor.** Metaphors can be useful often for condensing complex ideas into a single statement. They immediately evoke the characteristics associated with that metaphor and link those characteristics to your subject: '*We need to be less elephant and more tiger.*' This immediately conjures up two contrasting images: one of a heavy, immobile, inflexible giant, the other of a fast, powerful and deadly alternative. You don't need to say any more; people will know immediately where you want to go. This could give the following draft and final slides:

5 **Don't despair.** The key message is the very heart of your presentation. It deserves the best of your time and effort. Think carefully about its formulation. It is difficult to summarise complex ideas in a single sentence. Sometimes you think that the right words will never come. And perhaps they won't – or not at this precise moment. So leave it until later. In Phase 2, Step 5 ('Write your lead') you will be given new tools to help you.

IN SHORT

In this second important action you have set the goal for your presentation. You see clearly what you want to achieve and what your audience must know, feel and do. If possible, you have also formulated your key message as a powerful one-liner.

STEP 3

Plan your interaction

How do you want to achieve your objective?

Years ago, my team thought up a daring concept to improve the motivation and attitude of the staff at a large department store. The company had already tried several different ways to improve the customer friendliness of its people, but nothing seemed to work. The management now looked to us to provide effective training that would turn this unsatisfactory situation around.

What we came up with was something completely out of the box. It was not really a training, more a kind of 'big-brother' experience in a double-decker bus, in which the staff were central. We wouldn't tell them what to do; they would have to decide that for themselves.

We were asked to put forward our plan at a meeting of the management committee. But how could we convince the CEO and his team to agree to such an original, almost crazy, concept?

We decided that the best way was to let them try it for themselves. We persuaded them to hold the management meeting on the bus and, for a few hours, we put them in the same position their staff would be in – if they accepted our proposal.

Their reaction exceeded our wildest expectations. Not only were they extremely enthusiastic about our plan, but they also said that our radical approach had given them a better insight into the daily life of their staff and the problems they faced. The project was approved, even though our budget was much higher than they had originally foreseen.

For this presentation we used no more than five PowerPoint slides. And, looking back, even these weren't really necessary. Since then, more than 10 years have gone by, but, whenever I meet a member of that management committee, they still mention that day and our magical bus.

The type of interaction and the setting of your presentation have a huge impact on the final outcome. A good setting combines a number of different elements, which interact in a balanced manner:

- type of meeting;
- size of group;
- level and type of interaction;
- location;
- available time;
- information before and after;
- technical aids.

These are not so much steps in a process, but rather parts of a bigger whole. A bit like atoms, which, in spite of their 'freedom', still hang together in a meaningful pattern.

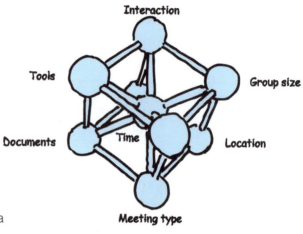

GIVE YOUR PRESENTATION TO THE RIGHT MEETING

Many meetings are a kind of 'presentation stew': totally different presentations are given to the same meeting. According to the American author Patrick Lencioni, the mixing of different subjects, each with a different type of interaction, is both ill-advised and counterproductive (Lencioni, 2004). Different types of interaction require a different mindset from your audience. Working out a strategic plan requires a totally different approach from the rapid processing of operational decisions.

This bears repeating: every type of interaction requires a different mindset and a different approach from your audience. Quick decisions, knowledge transfer, creative innovation and comprehensive analysis, etc. are not all the same and cannot be treated the same. Switching from one to the other is a real challenge – both for you and your listeners.

So, make sure, as far as possible, that you give your presentation in the right meeting, covering subjects that are, at least, similar. If this is not feasible, allow enough time to make the transition from one subject to another. Perhaps you can use a warm-up exercise to get your audience in the right frame of mind.

TAKE ACCOUNT OF THE GROUP SIZE

The size of the group has a major influence on your presentation. The greater the number of people, the lower the level of interaction and the more formal the atmosphere. Small groups are ideal, but not always possible or efficient. Presenting for a small group is much easier. For just a few people, you have less need of a perfect powerpoint. But this doesn't mean that you need to prepare any less thoroughly.

With larger groups, it is more difficult to adjust your presentation to your audience. Interaction is also harder to achieve. But it is still possible. Ask questions and allow collective answering ('hands up, please'). Or pick someone out of the audience with whom you can interact one-to-one. But avoid creating a kind of 'discussion club'; otherwise, you risk losing the rest of your audience.

BUILD IN OPTIONS FOR INTERACTION

The level of interaction will depend on the other setting factors. Are you going to give your presentation first and then finish with a round of questions or an open discussion? Or are you going to involve your audience during the actual presentation itself?

One thing is certain: interaction has many advantages. With interaction you attract people's attention, activate their existing knowledge and stimulate their working memory to make new combinations. As a result, your information is more likely to be processed into new knowledge and this knowledge will be rooted more deeply in their minds. The disadvantage is that you have less control over timing: make sure that your audience doesn't run away with your subject!

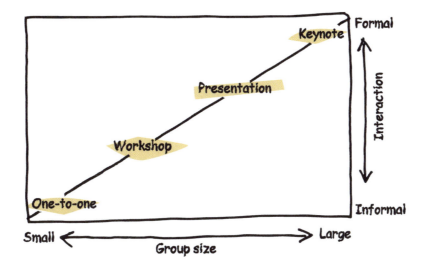

Tips to improve interaction with the audience

1 **Stand close to your audience.** Reduce the physical distance between you and them, and build emotional bridges. Move amongst the audience, if you can.

2 **Make eye contact.** Eye contact encourages people to respond.

3 **Ask questions.** But avoid discussions that jeopardise your timing or move too far away from your subject.

4 **Allow audience questions.** Decide in advance how much time or how many questions you can allow.

5 **Allow discussions in small groups.** Divide a large group into smaller discussion groups. Move from group to group, each time picking out a 'representative' who can summarise the opinions of his/her group as a whole.

6 **Use 'idea-parking'.** Use a flip chart to 'park' ideas. If the questions or the discussion start to deviate from your subject or objectives, put the idea in the parking area by writing it down. People will find it easier to let go of the idea if it has been recorded in some way.

CHOOSE AN APPROPRIATE LOCATION

It is not just the size of the group that affects the level of interaction; the size and layout of the location also play a role. This is not always something you can control, so sometimes you will have to adjust your approach to reflect the location's limitations. But, if you can choose your venue, remember to take account of the following points:

- Formal presentations are better in a 'theatre' setting (auditorium, hall, etc). You will be a bit further away from your audience, but that is acceptable in this context. If there is a middle aisle, you can walk along it whilst talking; this reduces the distance between yourself and the audience.

- If you need high interaction with a smaller group, use a U-shaped layout.

- If you need high interaction amongst the participants, use a table-based layout. With large groups, you can then create smaller 'islands' around which people can sit and discuss. This is more informal than sitting side by side in a long row and encourages people to talk.

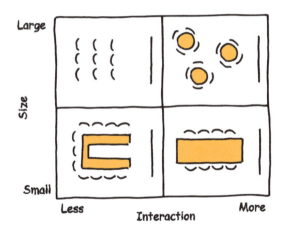

The actual physical location of your venue is another important factor. If the presentation is given in a place that has special memories or associations, people are more likely to remember what was said. If you have a unique message to communicate, choose an equally unique location. Do you have an engaging message for the whole workforce? Then it might be a good idea to give your presentation in the company's reception area. Every morning, when staff walk through the door, they will be reminded of your message. Even more so, if you put a banner in the foyer to strengthen the effect.

If you are giving a series of presentations on the same theme, it is better to do this in the same location. Your audience will then be able to remember better what was said last time, because the location stimulates the brain to bring back memories generated in the same location. Do not underestimate this effect. Research has shown that environmental factors relating to location can increase message recall by 50 per cent. This, for example, is why students are given lessons in the same subject often in the same room. If you always do history in classroom 4B, you associate history with that room – and this allows you to remember all those historical facts and figures with greater accuracy.

It depends on the context

Memories come back more easily when the sensory experience of the environment is similar to the moment when the memory was coded. Whenever we do or think something, our memory records the context. This is a far-reaching process: we can even associate smell with specific actions or events. And a similar context can later trigger those same memories.

Godden and Baddeley conducted a number of experiments to illustrate this (Godden and Baddeley, 1975). They asked the members of a diving club to memorise 25 unrelated words. Half of the group had to memorise the words on dry land; the other half whilst they were under water (via speaker system). Later, they were asked to recall as many of the 25 words as they could. Once again, they were split into two groups: one on land, one in the water.

The results were amazing. In the same environment, people were able to remember an average of 12 words. But, in a different environment, they were able to remember an average of only 8 words. In other words, a consistent environment allowed them to remember 50 per cent more!

**Mean number of words recalled
as function of learning and recall environment**

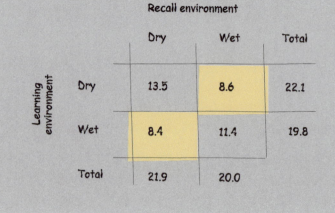

		Recall environment		
		Dry	Wet	Total
Learning environment	Dry	13.5	8.6	22.1
	Wet	8.4	11.4	19.8
	Total	21.9	20.0	

TAKE ACCOUNT OF THE AVAILABLE TIME

How much time do you need for your presentation? Or perhaps we should turn the question around: how much time have you been allocated? Most speakers and organisers consistently underestimate the time factor, resulting in a shortage of time at the end of the presentation. For this reason, prepare a presentation that takes up no more than 50 per cent of the allocated time. If you are given a time slot of an hour, prepare to speak for 30 minutes. Presentations tend to take longer than you think during preparation. And, if you have excess time, you can fill this up easily with questions, discussions, etc. Or just finish earlier. That is always better than rushing through the last part of your presentation at 100 miles an hour because time has run out.

PRE- AND POST-INFORMATION

The theory of the working memory discussed in Part I underlined the importance of prior knowledge. New knowledge is created by combining new information with what we already know. In other words, you need to adjust your presentation to reflect your audience's existing level of knowledge. Nothing is more frustrating than when one half of the audience knows much more about the subject than the other half. You will have more success if you can ensure that your entire audience starts with the same level of prior knowledge and is familiar with the terminology and concepts you will use.

WHAT TECHNICAL AIDS SHOULD YOU USE?

Most meeting rooms are equipped with a number of technical aids, such as a beamer, flip chart and sometimes even a smart board. There is a variety of other tools that can help you to make the most of your presentation. But first you need to be sure that they are indeed a help – not a hindrance.

Projection

Do not overlook this factor if slides play an important role in your presentation! Before putting lots of energy into making slides, check whether you will have an adequate projector and screen. On numerous occasions my beautiful slides have missed their effect totally because the meeting room was equipped with a flat screen that was too small and badly positioned. Remember, you don't always need slides. The use of a flip chart or white board often results in a more relaxed presentation.

Teleconferencing

The world is now a global village and more and more people are working remotely. As a result, videoconferencing is increasing in popularity. This has a major influence on your presentation.

Although many managers dislike videoconferencing, my experiences generally have been positive. It's true that you lose something in terms of interaction, but you more than make up for this with savings in travel time and cost. Here are some points to bear in mind.

- Videoconferencing works better when the participants already know each other.

- Make sure that everyone sees the same thing at the same time. This means that a videoconference is more effective than a teleconference without pictures. There are several good (and free) tools that allow you to show your presentation online.

- Communication always works more effectively if you can see the speaker. If possible, opt for a system where participants can see the speaker and the slides at the same time.

- The reverse is also true: it is better if the speaker can see his audience. The best videoconferencing systems foresee two-way vision.

Media naturalness

The theory of media naturalness says that communication is more efficient and effective when it corresponds with our natural way of communicating. This means that face-to-face communication works better than teleconferencing and a telephone call works better than an email.

This goes much further than many people think. For example, what we 'hear' is dependent partially on what we see. We do not hear only with our ears, but also – in part, at least – with our eyes. This is demonstrated in the so-called 'McGurk Effect', which shows that the visual observation of the speaker's mouth movement influences what we actually hear. McGurk filmed people saying certain words and sounds but dubbed the sound with other words and sounds. What then happens is that, when the sound tape lets you hear 'Bah', but the image shows someone saying 'Fa', you actually hear the non-audible 'Fa'.

I now work with many people from all over the world. One of them is a pleasant and intelligent woman of Chinese origin. We will call her Suzie. Suzie and I always talk in English. But Suzie's English pronunciation is not always easy to understand. Sometimes I need to concentrate very hard to work out what she is saying. But I have noticed several times that this is easier when I am talking to her face to face than on the telephone.

If we listen to someone we can see, it requires less mental effort from our brain to properly understand what is being said and it helps to focus our concentration.

Obviously this has consequences for your presentation. If a participant has difficulty in understanding the speaker, this leads to lower attention and a greater cognitive load. As a result, there is less cognitive capacity available to transform new information into new knowledge. This means that, as a speaker, you must always ensure that you are visible to your audience and that you speak slowly and clearly.

Electronic interaction

There are various systems on the market that allow participants to vote, give reactions or ask questions via their smartphone or some other device. These systems are useful only if you use them with care. They have a high 'gadget factor' and often distract attention from your key message. Even so, in some circumstances it can be interesting to gauge the immediate reaction of your audience in this manner ('how many of you think that ...'). The golden rule? Don't overdo it and keep it simple.

Tips for equalising your participants' level of prior knowledge

1 **Send out an information document in advance.** A pre-meeting document helps to create a level playing-field. It should cover the information and the terminology people must know to get the best out of your presentation. Unfortunately, my experience shows that only 30 per cent of participants take the trouble to even look at this document. And, the longer the text, the less likely it is to be read. So, keep it as short as meaningfully possible. To get around this problem, often I start my presentations with a quiz about the pre-information. This is always a success: it puts people in a good mood, whilst at the same time obliging them to read the documentation.

2 **Split the audience into groups.** This is the best solution when there are radically different levels of prior knowledge amongst the participants.

3 **Give an introductory presentation.** Split your presentation into two separate presentations. Ask the less well-informed part of your audience to come an hour earlier, so that you can fill in the gaps in their knowledge.

And what about handouts? It is always useful to give your listeners a document they can use to review your arguments after the presentation. Distribute this document right at the very end. If you do it earlier, half the audience will be flicking through the pages whilst you are still talking. But tell them in advance that a handout will be available. This will prevent everyone from scribbling down notes, when they should be listening.

Sending slides or handouts to the participants in advance is, generally, not a good idea. Some experts, such as Garr Reynolds (author of *Presentation Zen: Simple Ideas on Presentation Design and Delivery*), are radically opposed to it. Personally, I solve it this way: if a management committee asks to receive the slides before meetings, so that they can prepare themselves properly, I send them an easy-to-read slide deck with the full content of my presentation. However, I do not use those same slides during my presentation. Instead, I summarise my key message in one or two (new) slides, refer to the slides I have already sent, and then move on to an interactive discussion about the subject. Until now, this has always worked well.

IN SHORT

After identifying your objective and your target group, now you have fixed the setting and the strategy for your presentation, by finding the right combination of interaction, location, layout, group size, duration and prior information.

PHASE 2
THE LOGIC
What are you going to say?

CONTENT – LEAD – STRUCTURE

Online investing is hot. I was also thinking about giving it a try, so when I received an invitation from an online bank to attend a product presentation it didn't take me long to make up my mind. I filled in the answer form and pushed the Send button.

The bank had lined up one of their best sales people to give the presentation. And he was a born speaker. With great enthusiasm, he gave us an entertaining talk that managed to make a boring technical product sound sexy and exciting. Banking had never been so much fun!

Everyone in the room – myself included – was hanging on his every word. Like the true talent he was, he told his story with panache and style. There seemed no end to his brilliance. But that was precisely the problem: there was no end to it. He kept on quoting so many examples, special cases, exceptions and intelligent but complicated insights that his audience eventually lost the plot – and then lost interest.

During the reception afterwards, I heard the same comments being repeated. 'Fascinating, but it was all so complicated. It makes me uneasy. I am not really sure what to think.' And this from people who were used to dealing daily with investments and had arrived with every intention of trying the new product.

As a result, many potential customers were lost. Why? Because the abundance of arguments had installed uncertainty in their minds. In his enthusiasm, the speaker overwhelmed his audience by giving them too much and too complex information. He looked at online investment from so many different angles that his listeners no longer knew whether they were coming or going. And so they went ...

In this second phase we will be looking at what you want to say in your presentation. This is probably the hardest part of the entire process and deserves your full care and attention. In the preceding pages, you have decided who your presentation is for and what you want to achieve. You have also written out a powerful key message. Now the time has come to translate that key message into words and images that will convince your audience. This means collecting, selecting and ordering a wide variety of information. You will need to use both logical arguments and evocative illustrations. Or, to put it another way: objective content and subjective content.

- **Objective content:** To begin with, you need a core of objective data around which you can build up your reasoning. This is your logical, rational or objective content. It is the information you use to make the specific, reasoned arguments that will convince your listeners. You need to keep this content as simple as possible, by limiting it in quantity and giving it a clear structure. When I refer to 'the logic' of your presentation, this is what I mean: the objective, logical information – the 'knowledge' – you wish to communicate.

- **Subjective content:** To supplement and support your logic, you also need sensory, emotional, subjective content. These are the anecdotes and examples you use to illustrate your ideas. They are the details and emotions you need to attract the attention of your audience and fire their imagination. Subjective content makes sure that your logical content sticks in the memory. From now on, I will refer to this subjective content as 'the story' – which we will look at further in Phase 3.

FIRST THE LOGIC, THEN THE STORY

To give the necessary degree of structure to your presentation, first you need to build up your logical content. This will require you to use a mindset that is different from the one you will later use to write your story. For logical content, you need to use your capacity for logical thought. For the story, you need to use your empathic capability and your creative competencies. By using these mindsets separately, it is easier to make sure that neither of them gains the upper hand, which would ruin the balance in your presentation. So, remember: objective logic first, subjective story afterwards.

Of course, it is always possible that you will have creative insights whilst you are developing your logical content. Note them down on a separate sheet of paper and keep them until you need them for your story. The opposite is also true. If you discover a flaw in your logic whilst you are working on your story, go back a few steps and reorganise the objective content so that it forms a coherent whole.

Are you more of a logical thinker? You will need to devote plenty of attention to the actions in Phase 3. Creative readers should take extra care when dealing with Phase 2.

The importance of logic

All the evidence suggests that people base their decisions more on emotions than on logical argument. So what is the point of using logic in your presentation? Why not just play on the emotions of your audience?

The reason is simple: you cannot change emotions by using more emotion. Even though it is our emotions that finally decide things, reason also makes an important contribution. As human beings, we have learnt to apply a degree of control to our most primary emotions. We do this by testing these emotions against our reason. In other words, our ability to think logically prevents our primary emotions from making too many bad decisions. If this were not the case, we would all have cupboards full of very fashionable but useless stuff! It is logic that makes us human. It is our cognitive skills that allow us to recognise emotions and to guide and limit their effects, when necessary.

In important strategic meetings emotions are kept on a tight rein. Management committees usually want to see facts and figures. But it is different, for example, for a politician who wants to persuade the electorate to vote for him. In this case, he will score more heavily with images, metaphors and creative one-liners than with a correct, but boring, factual analysis.

KEEP IT SIMPLE

It surprises me, sometimes, how difficult and high-flown some presentations are, whereas it is always better to keep your message as simple as possible. This is supported by the theories of the working memory and cognitive load, which we discussed in Part I. Cognitive loading is the extent to which we burden our audience's capacity to think with the weight and complexity of our communication. You will achieve much more if you keep this weight within reasonable limits, so that your audience can concentrate fully on your message and not on the ballast.

Of course, 'keeping it simple' is relative and will depend on the prior knowledge of your listeners. If they are less familiar with your subject, you will need to aim for maximum simplification. But, if they are very knowledgeable, you must avoid simplifying matters too much. Managers could see this as a lack of respect: they don't expect to be treated like dummies and prefer to see presentations with a fair amount of detailed information. In general, it is advisable to steer a middle course, so that you don't frighten off your audience with either too much or too little information.

But most managers aren't Einsteins! Remember the curse of knowledge. Be aware that we all have the natural tendency to make our talk too complicated. Don't let this expertise tempt you into showing off how much you know. This is a lesson that many speakers forget. Most of the presentations I see contain too much information. Much too much.

Just a bit more complex, perhaps?

Research has shown that a highly educated and knowledgeable audience remembers better when it is provided with plenty of detailed information. In this context, education specialist Graham Cooper has written: 'When learners hold high levels of expertise in the content area, then the elements which their working memory may attend to are each, in and of themselves, large complex knowledge networks (high level schemas). Consequently, their working memory need only consider a few elements in order to hold all of the to-be-learned information in mind' (Cooper, 1998).

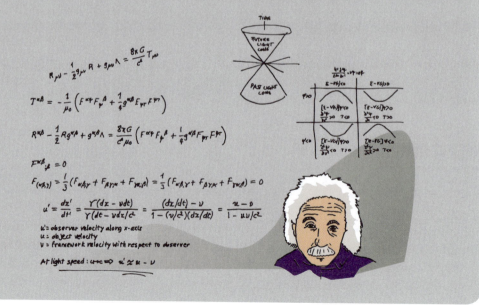

For example, the highly complex theory of relativity could be presented to a non-scientific audience with the famous equation e = mc² and an explanation of what would happen if a train could travel at the speed of light. For this audience, the detailed calculus that allowed Einstein to develop his theory would be incomprehensible gibberish. But, for a group of physicists, it would be child's play. The more your audience understands about your subject and the more intelligent they are, the more easily they can see the main thrust of your argument amongst a mass of details.

'Make everything as simple as possible, but not simpler.'

Albert Einstein

How do you do that?

How do you ensure that your message has the right degree of simplicity? You can do this by applying the following three steps in the further preparation of your presentation:

1 **Select the content.** List all the premises, arguments and information you want to include in your presentation.

2 **Write your 'lead'.** Make a very concise executive summary that contains the essence of the message you wish to pass on to your audience.

3 **Build your structure.** Draw up a logical, two-dimensional structure that links all your arguments together. This plan must reflect the logic of your reasoning and will form the basic framework of your presentation.

STEP 4

Select your content

Scrap the irrelevant, keep the essential

André, a friend of mine, has been a successful lawyer for years. We often exchange ideas about what it takes to make a good presentation. Because when you think about it, arguing a case in court is really just a presentation in a different form. One day we were discussing how much detail you need to use in your argument. André told me a story about when he was a young barrister, just starting his career.

He was defending a client whose case was pretty weak. The public prosecutor made a lengthy plea and demanded a heavy sentence. Things were looking pretty bad for the defendant and now it was André's turn. He stood up but spoke for less than five minutes (the prosecutor had droned on for half an hour). But whilst he was speaking, the judge opened the case file again and began looking through the documents. André had not expected this. It appeared that in just five minutes he had set the judge thinking again.

This was where André almost made a fatal mistake. Seeing that the judge was beginning to have his doubts, he began to summarise every possible argument he could think of, in the hope that this finally would swing the case in his client's favour. The judge raised a hand to stop him and looked at him over the top of his glasses. 'If I was you, young man, I would shut up now. If you carry on like this, you might persuade me to change my mind back again.' André closed his mouth and sat down. His client was acquitted.

'The greatest virtue of an orator is brevity!'

Jacques-Bénigne Bossuet (seventeenth-century bishop and legendary orator)

What lesson can you draw from this story for your presentation? A very important one; namely, that every piece of unnecessary information you give actually works against you. You must trust your audience to use their ears and their common sense to draw the right conclusions. Give them the essential information they need to do this – and then leave it at that.

But how do you arrive at this 'essential information'? The best way is to begin by gathering together all the usable material and in a second phase you sift through this material, until only the most important and useful elements are left.

I call this first phase the diverging phase. It involves you drawing up a longlist of everything you could say about your subject. This is followed by the second or converging phase, when you whittle down your longlist into a shortlist, by scrapping everything that is not strictly relevant.

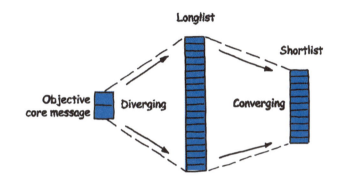

THE LONGLIST: THE DIVERGING PHASE

You don't draw up your longlist from scratch. You already have a subject, an objective and a key message from the work you did in the earlier phases. Using these as your starting point now you can search for all the information that may be useful for your presentation: arguments, theorems, propositions, suppositions, objections, ideas, statements of principle, etc. Write them all down: not in detail but in telegram style. Sometimes a single word will be enough.

No doubt you have been thinking about your presentation for some time. Probably you have a file – on paper or in your computer – with all the ideas and information you have already come across. Now is the time to open that file and examine its contents thoroughly. Put down everything in your longlist. But, remember that your own notes are not your only source. You can also find inspiration from a variety of other sources.

- **Brainstorming: alone or in a group.** We all know how brainstorming works. The most important thing is to refrain from judging: this will block the flow of ideas, whereas ideas are exactly what you need. Every idea is valid and potentially usable, so gather them all. The disadvantage of group brainstorming is the time it takes. Brainstorming alone is a good alternative, but is less interactive and therefore less diverse. Try to combine the best of both methods. First ask your team to brainstorm alone. Next, bring their ideas together in a group brainstorm.

Tips for better brainstorming

1 **Don't make the groups too big.** Between two and five people is ideal.

2 **Don't judge.** Note down anything and everything. Sometimes a stupid idea leads to a brilliant one. You can get rid of the rubbish during the shortlist phase.

3 **Quantity before quality.** Let everyone have their say and put down all the ideas in a list; the longer, the better.

4 **Think out of the box.** The ideas can be unrealistic, even absurd.

5 **Don't claim ownership.** Brainstorming ideas are the collective property of all involved, because you all build on each other's ideas.

6 **Note down everything.** Use a whiteboard or flip chart. This means that the ideas remain visible for a long time as a source of inspiration for new ideas. Keep the chart and take a photo of the board, so that nothing gets forgotten.

Brainstorming in a group has a further unexpected advantage. You forge a strong bond with the other participants. This means that they will be more favourable towards you and your ideas when you give your presentation.

- **Previous presentations.** Old presentations on the same subject can also give you a lot of useful information. But resist the temptation simply to copy the slides. First create your own content before checking to see if any of the old slides are usable. Don't do it the other way around! Rearranging old slides in a different order for a different purpose usually results in a poor presentation.

- **Question lists.** Draw up a list of all the questions you want to answer during the presentation. Use this list later as a checklist to see if your longlist is complete. Why? Who? What? When? Where? How?

- **Describe the problem.** If you are proposing a solution, write down everything related to the problem you are solving. What exactly is the problem? Where is it situated? How did it arise? Why wasn't it solved earlier?

- **All possible arguments.** If you ask for a decision, list all possible arguments for and against. The participants might need them to justify their choice both to themselves and to others.

- **Look at all possible dimensions.** In a business context, most subjects have a number of dimensions: financial, communication, technical, HR, logistics, planning, marketing, strategy, etc. Make sure you don't forget any of them.

- **Different ways of thinking.** Do you remember the HBDI and its different thinking styles on page 53? If you think in a logical, analytical manner, you may overlook the emotional and practical aspects of your subject. Try to think in each of the four styles and develop arguments that are appropriate to each one.

Using all these sources of information, eventually you will arrive at a longlist. This list is wholly unstructured, but that is not a problem at this stage.

Manipulation with good intentions

Presentations are about influencing and convincing people. There are many arguments that can help you to achieve this. However, it is important to be fair and to avoid being seen as manipulative: people could hold this against you. But, as a long as you are honest and sincere, there are lots of things you can do to get your audience on your side. In his book *Influence: Science and Practice*, Robert Cialdini described six ways you can have an impact on people's behaviour (Cialdini, 2000):

1 **Reciprocity.** Give a present to your audience, either literally or figuratively. If you show people what you have done for them, they will feel obliged to do something back in return.

2 **Commitment and consistency.** People want to be consistent with their own ideas and opinions. As soon as they have committed themselves to something, it is difficult for them to change their minds or back down. This means that if you can get a 'yes' answer to part of what you want, it is then easier to progressively obtain a 'yes' for all the other parts – particularly if that first 'yes' was made publicly.

3 **Social proof.** People easily allow themselves to be persuaded to do what others do. Give them evidence of this during your presentation. Show what other departments, competitors, industries, etc. are doing.

4 **Liking.** People support or follow the people they like. Everything that can make you more sympathetic in your audience's eyes therefore will work to the benefit of your presentation.

5 **Authority.** People are more ready to believe someone they regard as an authority figure. The power of a uniform to impress has been known for centuries. Show your audience why you are an authority in your domain or how authority figures support your ideas.

6 **Scarcity.** People want to have things that are scarce. If you can show your audience that your proposal is unique, they will be more ready to follow you, for fear of missing out on the possible benefits.

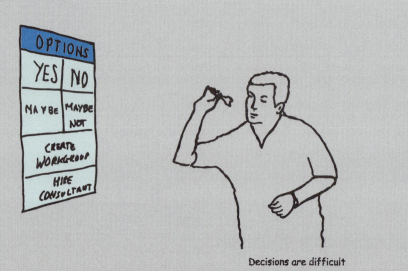

Decisions are difficult

Decisions are difficult

The objective of a presentation often is to make a decision. But decisions are difficult. And people do not always decide in the same way. Try to find out how your audience reaches its decisions or suggest your own decision-making process.

Eldar Shafir, a psychologist at Princeton University, has distinguished four methods for reaching a decision (Shafir et al., 1993):

1 **The standard procedure.** This is the simplest method. There are proposals on the table to deal with a problem, the type of problem is well-known and the company always evaluates problems of this kind in the same way. In other words, there is a fixed approach with fixed criteria, templates and procedures. This is often the case with budgetary discussions, project planning, etc. Make sure that all the elements of the standard procedure are included in your presentation.

2 **The quantitative approach.** You see this approach often with economic decisions. All arguments are condensed into a single numerical value. Companies often choose the option with the highest return on investment (ROI). Viewed mathematically, this is the best choice. The problem is that you are not always comparing like with like. If you have a choice between two similar apartments, and if apartment A costs €1,300 and apartment B costs €1,000, you will choose apartment B. But what if apartment A is in a better area? What is the price for a better area?

3   **The qualitative approach.** With this approach you identify all possible arguments that can have an influence on the decision. You then make a summary of 'for' and 'against'. You reach your final decision by balancing the pros and cons of the two columns. This method can take account of less tangible factors, such as ethics, risk and company values. For this reason, it comes closer to the way people naturally make decisions.

4   **Affective judgement.** Irrational, affective arguments influence the decision-making process much more that people often realise. In these cases it becomes more difficult to predict how and why a particular choice will be made. The final decision often depends on the person taking it or the manner in which the choice is presented. Because you have less control over the outcome, it is better to avoid this method.

THE SHORTLIST: THE CONVERGING PHASE

During the preparation of your longlist you will have collected a huge amount of information. But you won't need to use it all, because too much information has a negative effect on the decision-making process. Unnecessary detail draws attention away from the key message and increases indecisiveness. For this reason, we now need to separate the wheat from the chaff. In other words, we are going to turn our longlist into a shortlist.

Start by removing all the duplications; the ideas that are repeated more than once, possibly in different versions. Keep the strongest formulation.

The rest of your choices will be more difficult. What do you leave in and what do you take out? There is only one way to do this: you must always refer back to your objective and key message. Everything that fails to support your key message must be removed. Everything that does not bring you closer to your objective is a waste of time.

The only exception to this rule relates to premises and suppositions that contradict your objective and key message. Counter-arguments should be left in your shortlist. If your audience thinks you are hiding something, it will turn against you. So don't avoid counter-arguments. In fact, I would suggest that you discuss them early on in your presentation. You can be certain that there will always be someone in your audience who can see the weak points in your argument. As long as he thinks you are trying to pull the wool over his eyes, his cognitive brain will be trying to think of ways to 'expose' you in the question-and-answer session. As a result, he will be listening with only one ear. But, if he sees that you are self-critical and are not afraid to confront difficult issues, he will devote his full attention to what you have to say.

How long is a shortlist?

A shortlist is usually less than 50 per cent of the longlist. This is not easy to achieve, since it means you will have to leave out lots of 'interesting' information. But you must be ruthless: kill your darlings! It is essential to avoid cognitive overload amongst your audience. Because this would reduce their ability to process your key message, so that you may fail to reach your objective.

If there is information that is not strictly necessary for your objective or your key message but that you think the audience really needs to know, you may need to look again at the objective and the key message. Go back to Phase 1 and see if your key message can be reformulated, so that the information now fits.

The end result will be a shortlist of propositions, arguments and conclusions that support your objective and on which you can now further build your presentation.

How many alternatives should you suggest?

Making a decision often involves more than a single choice option. But how many different options should you put forward? Imagine that you have tested seven ideas to boost the sales of a particular product. You have gathered a huge amount of data and the management now wants you to present the results. What are you going to do? Discuss the results for all seven options? Or just the best two? Or just the best one?

The more choice options a person is given, the more difficult it becomes to make a decision. For this reason, it is better not to suggest too many alternatives. The management team knows that you have investigated seven options, but it is wiser to let them choose between just two. In this way, the decision will be made more quickly and with less confusion. If you give them seven options, there is a much greater chance that they will end up tying themselves in knots.

Tips to make decisions easier

In my experience this is a good strategy for making the choice and decision making that much easier:

1 Mention the number of alternatives you have considered.

2 Give more details about two or three of the alternatives.

3 Say clearly which alternative you prefer.

4 Justify your preference.

5 Have back-up material available:

 – A list of all the alternatives (including those not detailed in the presentation).

 – At least one reason per alternative to explain why you rejected them.

More choice means more problems

Dr Donald Redelmeier (a physician-researcher in Toronto who often dares to question preconceived notions in the medical world) and Eldar Shafir (Professor in Psychology and Public Affairs at Princeton University), carried out research on medical decision making and how multiple options influence decisions. They conducted an experiment with two groups of doctors (Redelmeier and Shafir, 1995). The first group was given a choice to prescribe or not prescribe a particular medicine for osteoarthritis. Seventy-two per cent decided to prescribe it.

The second group was given an additional option: they could prescribe the medicine, not prescribe it, or prescribe an alternative medicine. The result was that only 53 per cent prescribed either the medicine or the alternative. Redelmeier concluded from this that, if you offer more options, you actually reduce the likelihood that any decision will be made. The experiment was repeated with different medical conditions, but the results were always broadly the same.

More choice makes it more difficult to decide

STEP 4
CONTENT

How many arguments should you use?

Remember the salesman of the online bank who puts off customers with too many arguments (page 73)? Research supports this example, adding that too much information actually reduces the willingness of people to vote for a particular proposal, even if the extra arguments did nothing to detract from the validity of the proposal itself. So there seems to be a tipping point: adding arguments will make it more probable that the audience accepts your view, until a certain point where adding even more arguments will reduce that probability.

The question you therefore need to answer is: how detailed should you make your argument? Here are some tips:

- If you are offering a choice between different alternatives, **focus on the differences**. Decisions usually are made more quickly when the differences are clear. For this reason, it is advisable to highlight the differences between your proposed options. Spend much less time on information about their common characteristics.

- Should you use **many or few supporting arguments**? Imagine that you have seven arguments to support a particular decision. Order them from strong to weak. Would you use all seven? Or only the best three?

- To a large extent, this will depend on the **prior knowledge of your audience**. If your audience is knowledgeable, you can add additional arguments without risk, since your listeners are capable of interpreting them and will allow them to influence their decision accordingly.

  But if your audience is not familiar with the subject, you should use **only the most obvious arguments**. Their brain is already fully occupied in trying to understand the basic point you wish to make; adding extra, less important arguments will only serve to cloud their judgement. And, as soon as there is uncertainty, even if it is not strictly relevant, the resistance to making a decision of any kind will grow.

How many cards do you play?

Uncertainty is your enemy

Every form of uncertainty, even if that uncertainty is not relevant for your subject, leads to indecision.

Amos Tversky is an American psychologist and pioneer in the field of cognitive psychology. He carried out a series of tests on students to see how the provision of additional information influenced their decision making (Tversky and Shafir, 1992).

A group of students was offered a package holiday at a very low price. They received this offer the day before their exam results were announced. If they didn't sign up immediately for the holiday, they had the opportunity to do so again two days later (after the results were known) at the same low price, but, to be allowed this delay, they had to pay a $5 advance that would not be refunded.

A small group of students knew their exam results in advance and so were better informed than the others. As far as this group with prior knowledge was concerned, the exam results seemed to have little influence on their decision whether or not to go on holiday:

- 54 per cent of those who passed their exams immediately accepted the low-cost offer.
- 57 per cent of those who failed their exams did the same.

Less than one third chose to delay their decision.

And, what about the students who didn't know their results in advance? Sixty-one per cent paid the $5 supplement so that they could postpone their decision until after the results were known, even though passing or failing had no influence on their final choice.

Who signs up for the holiday and who pays $5 to postpone the decision?

	Result unknown	Passed	Failed
Signs up	32%	54%	57%
Does not sign up	7%	16%	12%
Pays $5 to postpone	61%	30%	31%

Conclusion? Although the actual result (pass/fail) had no impact on their holiday plans, the uncertainty about the result meant that more people were unwilling to take an immediate decision to sign up for the low-cost deal.

IN SHORT

Now you have made a list of the objective content you want to include in your presentation. On the one hand, you made sure that you forgot nothing and on the other hand you scrapped everything that did not contribute directly towards achieving your objective. This was a difficult balancing act, which required courage, since you had to make choices to leave out a number of interesting elements: you had to 'kill your darlings' – and that is never easy.

STEP 5
Write your lead
Begin with your conclusion

Years ago, when I was looking to recruit new staff, I met Jess. She was tall, blonde and 28 years old. A good-looker, but not fashionably dressed and she gave a bit of a clumsy first impression. What's more, she had obviously been eating garlic the night before and, as for her hair ... In short, a bit of a disappointment, I thought.

At least her CV spoke in her favour. After her initial poor start, she came on strong and, at the end of the conversation, I decided to let her go through to the next phase of the selection process. My colleagues thought she would fit in well with the company, and so she was given a job. She quickly proved that we had made the right decision.

But for a long time I found her unpleasant company. Whilst everyone else was praising her to the heavens, I remained cool and non-committal. Which just goes to show how an unfair, negative first impression can last for a long, long time.

'You never get a second chance to make a first impression.'

Making a good first impression: we have all heard a thousand times how important it is. The impression and emotions of that first moment of contact are deeply etched in our brain and are almost impossible to eradicate. This is not only true for personal contact, but applies equally to books, films and ... presentations. If you can't grab your audience with your opening remarks and your first slide, you might have lost them for good.

Five minutes: that's about the length of time you have to get your audience on your side. If you can't interest them during that brief opening period, they will turn off mentally.

The film industry has found an answer to this problem. They call it 'the hook'. This is the scene at the beginning of the film that has to get the audience on the edge of their seats. Once they are there, you have a chance to keep them there. Of course, the rest of the film has to match up to the gripping start. But, without the hook, you can forget it. Game over. So take a leaf out of the film makers' book: make sure you begin your presentation with a really good 'hook'.

BEGIN WITH THE ESSENCE OF YOUR STORY

There is, however, an important difference between a film and a presentation. A film-maker is trying to make his audience warm to his film, without giving away the ending. But, in a presentation, you need to communicate the essence of your story early on. For this reason, the comparison with the 'lead' in journalism is, perhaps, more appropriate.

The lead is the opening paragraph of an article that grabs the reader's attention, but also succinctly summarises the content. It always includes the key message. If you fail to do this, you risk 'burying' your message in the detail of your text.

There are three reasons why your lead should contain the key message:

1 **Attention fades.** People's attention is highest at the start of your presentation. No matter how hard you try to maintain this level of attention, it will decline gradually as you talk. In other words, it is inevitable that your audience will 'miss' part of your message. But, with a powerful early 'lead', you will have said already the things that are most important. And, if you do it well, these things will stick in the memory.

2 **Time is limited.** Especially if you are not the only person making a presentation, often you will be confronted with a shortage of time. The speaker before you might overrun or you might misjudge the time yourself. When this happens, you need to cut things from the end of your presentation. But, if that is where you were planning to give your key message, you are in big trouble.

3 **The human brain likes to see the big picture.** If we can see where an argument is leading, we find it easier to understand. Our working memory prefers to focus first on the big picture. The details can come later.

So don't do as a film director does – in business presentations it is better to start with your conclusion, and then build up your arguments to support it. There are only two scenarios – neither of which is common – where you can keep your proposal to the end:

1 **When you are expecting brutal opposition.** In this case, it might be wiser first to explain the situation clearly and develop arguments at length, so that people have time to change their minds before coming to a conclusion.

2 When you are solving a 'mystery'. Something that everybody is passionate about, so that they are all dying to know the answer. In this case, there is enough tension to save your conclusion until the end.

But, in all other cases, follow the golden rule: play your most important cards early on in the game.

How long should a lead be? Five minutes is usual. Sometimes it can be a bit longer, if you need to give background information. But make sure that it is not longer than 10 minutes. You will not be able to hold your audience's attention for more than this. After 10 minutes, people start to show the first signs of listening fatigue. After 15 minutes, some will have turned off completely.

STEP 5
LEAD

Keep it short

A major financial institution decided that it wanted to change its internal meeting culture, so that it could improve its overall efficiency levels. I was invited as an external expert to observe some of their meetings. One of them was held in the magnificent hall of a mansion house, complete with wood-block floor, crystal chandeliers, oak panelling and a giant mahogany table. But the conference facilities were almost as antique as the rest of the interior, with a portable beamer and an old-fashioned roll-out screen!

As an observer, I watched the reactions of the participants. One presentation was scheduled to last 45 minutes and I could see that, during the opening phase, the speaker's proposal was well received. It could have been approved immediately. But this was something the speaker himself failed to notice. Forty-five minutes came and went, and still he kept on talking. By then, his audience's attention was everywhere except on the presentation. Some were playing with their smartphones; others made excuses to leave the room. It was painful to watch. After 55 minutes, the speaker finally sat down.

Did they let the man overrun out of politeness? Or was this just their habit?

The proposal was accepted finally. But at what cost? Thirty senior managers listened to 50 minutes of unnecessary explanation. That represents a time investment of 25 wasted hours. Why did no one – the chairman for example – cut in? It was clear to me that the speaker could have had his proposal approved after just his 'lead'. So why ramble on for another 45 minutes? Why do we always feel that we have to use up all the available time?

THE ABC OF A GOOD LEAD

What are the characteristics of a good lead? One way to find out is to read *The Pyramid Principle* by Barbara Minto (Minto, 1981), a former consultant at McKinsey and then leader of her own company, Minto International. In this and the next step (Build your structure) I will be using a number of her ideas, adapted for presentations. The book itself applies these ideas more fully and more strictly. Although written in 1981, it is still applicable today and I encourage everyone to read it.

The lead is made up of three separate elements: **Situation – Complication – Solution (SCS)**. Or you can look at it as four elements: **Situation – Complication – Question – Answer (SCQA)**.

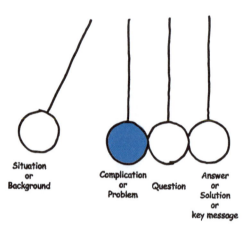

Situation or background

This is where you lay the foundations for your presentation. The situation is the framework in which you present. It is the place where you make contact with the shared knowledge of your audience. You get your background information from the shortlist you made earlier. You use all the premises and arguments you know are familiar to your listeners and that you are confident they will agree with. This underlines again why it is important to know your audience.

Because the audience is already aware of this information, you can keep it short and high level. One slide and five minutes is usually enough to summarise your situation.

Starting with the situation has many advantages:

- You create the right context for the further development of your arguments. Reminding people of the situation serves to load information from the long-term memory into their working memory. You bring the knowledge they need to understand your proposal back to the surface of their minds.

- Everything you summarise now doesn't need to be mentioned again later on. This gives you more time to develop and support your key message.

- Sometimes you are not certain what the audience knows. When you sketch the situation, this will become obvious. Do you see blank faces or nods of approval? If you are still not certain, ask openly for confirmation.

- Asking for confirmation has another advantage. If your audience openly agrees with your background information, this makes it harder for them to change their minds later in the presentation (see 'commitment' on page 81). You have got them in a positive 'yes' mood and this creates goodwill. There is now a greater chance that they will buy the rest of your arguments.

Complication or problem

From the author Simon Sinek, we have already learnt to ask the 'why' question: Why are you making this presentation? If you can't find a clear answer to this question, then it is better not to give the presentation. However, usually there is an answer and often it comes in the form of a problem that needs to be solved, or a complication or issue that needs attention:

COMPLICATION
You have discovered something interesting
We have run into difficulties
We might run into difficulties
Something has changed
Something needs to be decided
You are asked to report on a status

Although all these are not, strictly speaking, complications, from now on I will refer to the reason for your presentation as 'the complication'.

(Key) question

The complication always results in a further question – the key question of your presentation:

COMPLICATION	KEY QUESTION
You have discovered something interesting	**What is it?**
We have run into difficulties	**How can we solve the complication? What are the consequences?**
We might run into difficulties	**How can we avoid it?**
Something has changed	**What are the consequences?**
Something needs to be decided	**What must we decide? What are the options?**
You are asked to report on a status	**Should we be worried? Are we making progress?**

And, just as you formulated your objective and key message in clear and unambiguous terms, you now need to do the same with the complication and the key question. If you fail to do this, there is a risk that your presentation will remain vague. Ask this key question explicitly during your presentation.

Answer, solution or key message

The key message is the cornerstone of your presentation, the central element to which everything is linked. You have described the key message already in the first phase, but now it must be put forward as the answer to your key question, which was derived from your complication. If you had difficulty defining your key message in the first phase, this should be easier now that you have a key question to base it on:

COMPLICATION	KEY QUESTION	KEY MESSAGE
You have discovered something interesting	What is it?	**The essence of your discovery**
We have run into difficulties	How can we solve the complication? What are the consequences?	**A proposed solution** **A summary of the consequences**
We might run into difficulties	How can we avoid it?	**The proposed action (if necessary)**
Something has changed	What are the consequences?	**A summary of the consequences**
Something needs to be decided	What must we decide? What are the options?	**A summary of the options**
You are asked to report on a status	Should we be worried? Are we making progress?	**A reassuring message or a summary of areas for improvement**

If it transpires that your key message does not give an answer to your key question, something clearly is wrong. Go back to the first phase and adjust your key message accordingly.

A supermarket in difficulties

The senior management of a major supermarket chain was at its wit's end. In 10 years its product range had changed dramatically. New brands and white-label products had multiplied, and there was a whole new spread of financial, internet and mobile telephone products. The number of commercial actions imposed by the HQ on the branches had also soared, but the organisational changes to cope with this had been minimal. The job description of the store managers remained the same as it always had been. This led to tension. Unwittingly, the overloaded managers began to run their supermarkets less and less efficiently. The number of complaints about pressure of work increased. Many suffered from burn-out.

Within the company, there were some who thought that hard work – up to 60 hours per week – was part of the job. Others thought the store managers were setting the wrong priorities. A third group even thought that the wrong managers had been recruited.

Our company was asked to make an analysis of the situation. We came to the conclusion that the job of the store managers was too demanding. We proposed transferring some of their tasks to other personnel at the same sales point, with several other tasks being redirected back to the HQ. This would allow the managers to devote more time to their key task: running their supermarkets, supervising their staff and keeping the customers happy.

What lead would you write for this story? We came up with the following summary:

1 **Situation:**
   - During the last 10 years the number of products and commercial actions has risen dramatically; at the same time the role descriptions have remained the same.
   - The store managers are increasingly unhappy; many are suffering from burn-out.
   - There are different possible explanations.
   - An independent study has been made.

2 **Complication:**
   You have reached the point where you need to take action.
   Key question: what do you need to change?

3 **Key message:**
   Reduce the workload on store managers by redistributing some of their responsibilities.

IN SHORT

You have just written down the essence of your message. This will be your way of immediately involving your listeners in your presentation. This lead is always made up of the same three elements:

- A summary of what everyone already knows: the **situation** or **background**.
- The reason why you are giving the presentation: the **complication** and the **key question**.
- The answer to the key question: your **key message**.

By giving the lead at the start of your presentation, you will attract the full attention of your audience and anchor the most important things in their mind, allowing you to keep the rest of your content relatively short and making your reasoning easier for people to understand.

STEP 6

Build your structure

Create an impeccable, scalable logic

Some time ago I was invited to give a series of workshops for the senior management of a pharmaceutical company. I showed them the way to structure their information logically in a pyramid structure and demonstrated how this technique can be applied in practice. One of the participants asked me if I could help him to draw a structure chart for his own job, which – I had to admit – was extremely complex.

I suggested that first he should have a go himself, and that we would look at it during the next workshop. He duly brought his homework with him, and I suggested he should try explaining it to his other nine colleagues around the table. He drew the structure on a flip chart and added some explanation. The reactions of his colleagues were unexpected. 'That's amazing! Now I understand what you do. It used to seem so complex. But suddenly it has all become clear.' Everything that the man had tried to explain about his job in the past had come across as an incomprehensible, amorphous mass (and mess) of overcomplicated information. But now the fog had lifted, suddenly all was clear ... He admitted even himself: 'I have never looked at my job in such a way. But now I have a better insight into all its different aspects and how they are connected.'

The shortlist you made earlier contains lots of useful ideas, propositions, suppositions, conclusions and arguments, all connected to each other in many different ways. But this material lacks order. For your listeners – like in our example above – this will also be an incomprehensible mass of information. It is now your task to bring order to this mass, so that it has a logical structure. But how exactly do you do this?

Read the following text.

'On the horizon stood a house on a hill. To its left, the crowns of two weather-worn oaks nodded gently back and forth in the wind, like two old friends remembering old times. They sought each other's support, but also needed help from a concrete pylon, which some unromantic soul had planted directly between them, its wires reaching out towards the house like some sinister spider's web. The landscape was split by the scar of an ugly asphalt road, which branched off to the left and right. One fork led past the house. The other snaked its way over the horizon, disappearing into nothingness.

A stork had built its nest in the house's chimney. A woman was climbing up a ladder to remove its tangled mesh of twigs, mud and feathers. Autumn was coming, and they would soon need to light the fire ...'

What happens in your head when you read this text? No doubt you visualise the description in your mind, forming a picture in which all the different elements are included and are given a proper place. Well, this is exactly what happens in the minds of the audience during your presentation. They form a mental image of all the information you give them and of the relationship between its different components. And, as the speaker, it is important for you to determine exactly how this mental image looks.

This means, of course, that first you need to construct your own image. In other words, you need to take the mass of information lying on your desk, then sort it and structure it in a logical, visual two-dimensional framework.

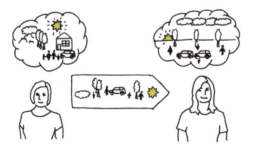

Why does your message need a logical structure?

HOW CAN YOU DEVELOP A CLEAR STRUCTURE?

Many efforts have already been made to develop an instrument that allows you to transform complex ideas into a clear structure. Some of them even have been issued in software form. The best-known, probably, is the mindmap. Tony Buzan, who claims to be the inventor, registered the trademark 'mindmap' and a TV series on the BBC promoted his ideas in the 1970s (Buzan and Buzan, 1993).

Even so, there is a good variety of other structuring tools. The mindmap might be the most widely used, but my preference goes to Barbara Minto's 'Pyramid Principle', which I mentioned earlier. The problem with mindmaps is that you have a tendency to add more and more information, whereas your job as a speaker is to limit and simplify information. A mindmap is (as Buzan himself puts it) 'a Swiss Army knife for the brain': it serves many purposes. But a really good chef uses a different knife for each task.

Mindmapping is fine when you are brainstorming or drawing up your longlist. But, in this phase of your presentation preparation, you are much better off using the Minto Pyramid Principle.

Combine ideas into meaningful clusters

The idea of grouping things that belong together into clusters is a method that we have developed as a species to overcome the limitations of our working memory.

An example will illustrate what I mean. Read the following row of numbers twice. Then cover the row and try to write down as many numbers as you can remember.

| 4 | 4 | 7 | 8 | 1 | 4 | 0 | 7 | 2 | 4 | 8 |

How well did you do? Most of the people I have tried it with get no further than six or so (an average of 6.4, to be precise). Now do the same with the next row:

44   781   407   248

How many did you remember this time? Like most people, you probably scored eight or nine this time; 50 per cent better than the score of six just a minute ago. What is the reason for this sudden improvement? The answer is simple: you grouped together a disparate set of symbols into more manageable clusters. It is easier to remember numbers in clusters of two to four than individually. That's why we write phone numbers like this.

Clustering is also a technique that you can use to your benefit in your presentation. Try this second test with letters instead of numbers. Once again, see how many you can remember:

| IT | VB | BCT | FLB | ANH | SPH | EMI | 5M | PS |

It's much harder this time, isn't it? Are you surprised? After all, the letters are in groups of two and three, so they should be easier to remember. Now try again with these same letters grouped differently:

| ITV | BBC | TFL | BA | NHS | PHE | MI5 | MPS |

Depending on where you live, it requires much less effort to remember these letter combinations. If you know these acronyms, these clusters of letters are already lodged in your long-term memory. What's more, each of the clusters has a meaning so that, when your brain recognises the cluster, it also recalls this meaning. (In this instance, these are UK organisations of public interest.)

You can even take this a stage further by grouping the acronyms at a higher level:

UK organisations of public interest							
Television companies		Public transport organisations		Health organisations		Safety and security organisations	
ITV	BBC	TFL	BA	NHS	PHE	MI5	MPS

You can do the same with the information in your shortlist. Group these pieces of information together into logical and meaningful clusters and then integrate them into a higher, even more meaningful, category. Keep doing this until finally you end up with just one idea at the top. And, hey presto! Without knowing it you have built a pyramid!

USE THE MINTO PYRAMID

Barbara Minto has drawn up a number of guidelines that can turn a pyramid into a powerful instrument for structuring messages. Her Pyramid Principle provides you with the weapons you need to transform your content into a clear, unambiguous and logical unity. One of the beauties of this model is, as you will see later, that it allows you to shorten your presentation at a glance. The model originally dates from 1981 and is still widely used today, more or less in its original form. With one or two minor adjustments, it is the perfect way to provide a logical structure to your presentation.

In practice, I have noted that presenters usually feel most comfortable when they use a combination of the Pyramid Principle, which offers a conceptual-relational structure, and a secondary linear-hierarchical structuring tool, which requires less effort and is sufficient for ordering the lower-level and back-up information.

A pyramidal presentation structure reduces the cognitive load

I have explained how the human brain groups and abstracts information in pyramidal structures. In 1996 Graham Hitch published a scientific article in which he demonstrated how the grouping of information affects memory recall (Hitch, 1996). His experiments showed that people remember 30 per cent more, if the spoken information is grouped into logical groups. This is even 60 per cent for visual information.

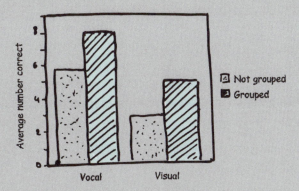

Grouping of information significantly improves recall

This effect can be explained as follows: If, as the 'sender', you fail to group your information, the receiver automatically will try do it himself. However, this involves a degree of cognitive load, so that the receiver's working memory is busy grouping the information and therefore can process less of the incoming information.

This proves, beyond doubt, the importance of grouping the information in your presentation into logical blocks. However, there is also another reason to do it as a presenter, rather than leaving it to your listeners. The way you group the information also gives it meaning. If you let others do it, they might give different meaning to the same information. And that is not what you want!

HOW DO YOU BUILD A MINTO PYRAMID?

You can build a Minto Pyramid on a sheet of paper, a whiteboard or a flip chart. It's up to you – as long as you have plenty of space, and an easy way to amend and adjust. Don't expect to get your pyramid right at the first attempt. You will need to change it many times before you finally produce a version that reduces your thoughts to their simplest and clearest form.

You can build your pyramid in two different ways:

1 **Top-down.** You begin with your key message and work downwards via question and answer towards the fine detail at the bottom.

2 **Bottom-up.** You take your shortlist and start grouping information logically. At the top of each group you write a summarising idea. Repeat this process with the different groups until you end up with just the key message.

If you are a true master of your subject, the top-down method is the quickest. This method works as follows.

The key message

Begin with the 'lead' that you wrote earlier. See what you noted down for the **situation**, **complication** and **key question**, and **answer** or **key message**. Use these elements to draw the top of your pyramid.

Let's have a look at an example. Imagine that you want to convince half of your colleagues to come to work by bicycle. Your situation is:

- the company is located on the edge of town;
- most of the staff live less than 10 km from their place of work;
- 80% come by car;
- 10% use carpooling;
- 5% use public transport;
- 5% walk or cycle.

Your 'complication' is that we have never considered to do it differently. The key question linked to this is: '**What can we change?**'

The answer is, perhaps: '**Half of us could come to work by bike.**' This becomes your key message.

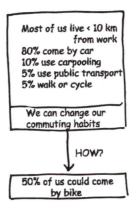

Questions and answers

Now, you need to think about the questions this will raise in the minds of your audience. Try to put yourself in their shoes. Write down the main question you think they would ask when hearing your key message.

The most obvious of these question is 'Why should we change?' Note down the question under your key message and, underneath, draw different boxes with different answers to the question:

- It is better for the world.
- It is better for you.
- It is better for the company.

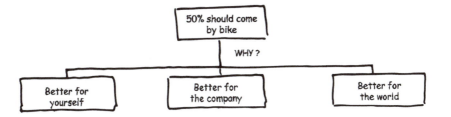

Under these three categories, you can easily sum up all the advantages of cycling to work.

Now the first level of your pyramid is complete. Now you can dig deeper and go into more detail. Work in exactly the same manner. For each of the answers you wrote down in the category boxes, try to find a follow-up question and give the different answers to this new question. Note the answers down in new boxes, as shown in the diagram below. In this way, you will build up a logically constructed pyramid, which will form the structure for your entire presentation.

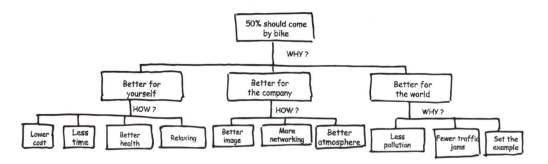

Use just one question at a time

Usually it is possible to ask a number of questions with each of the statements in, but make sure you ask only one: the most important one. You must avoid the mistake that many people make, when they put down a series of questions under their key message. Instead of six meaningless questions, you now give three powerful messages.

THE WRONG WAY	THE RIGHT WAY
Title	**Title**
The bike for commuting to and from work	**Half of us could come to work by bike**
• **What** is the problem?	(Why?)
• **Why** must we change?	• It is better for the world.
• **How** will we bring about the change?	• It is better for you.
• **Who** do we need to consider?	• It is better for the company.
• **When** will we start?	
• From **where** can you come with your bike?	

This first level of your pyramid will form the basis of your summary or agenda slide, which will reappear a number of times in your presentation.

By restricting yourself to one question, you build a much simpler and much clearer line of argument with a lower cognitive load. As a result, your proposal will be much easier for your audience to understand. And all those other questions? Don't worry – they will be dealt with later, at a lower level of abstraction.

Note that in each box I have put assertions or statements, rather than a single word. For example, write 'Better for your health', and not just 'health', which doesn't really mean very much to anyone. Statements increase the conversational feel of your presentation. They also prevent you from using too many platitudes, like 'Let's take a look at health'. Instead, you hear yourself say: 'It's better for your health, so let's see why'. In this second version you take a position and announce a message. Much stronger!

Backwards and forwards referencing

Your pyramid is a simplification of reality. By putting information in a pyramid structure, you reduce a totality of complex relationships to a simple two-dimensional map. This map does not show all the relationships between the assertions. For this reason, sometimes you will need to refer to an item elsewhere in the map by means of backwards or forwards referencing.

You can do this on the map by drawing an arrow from one item to the other.

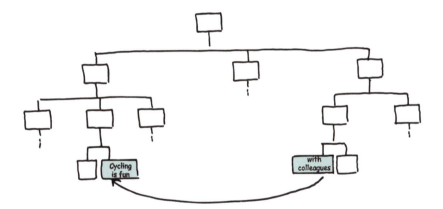

Backwards referencing gives an extra dimension

When do you stop?

In practice, most pyramids consist of three to five layers. You can stop when you think you have used enough material to make your point. Collect your remaining information in an appendix. You may or may not use this information during your presentation, so keep it as back-up.

If you have sufficient time, you can put that extra information in a pyramid. That is always better. But if you don't, just draw a hierarchically ordered list and attach it to the bottom of your main pyramid. This does not conform strictly to the Minto principles but, in view of the lesser importance, this really is not needed.

We can now distinguish three different levels in the pyramid we have made.

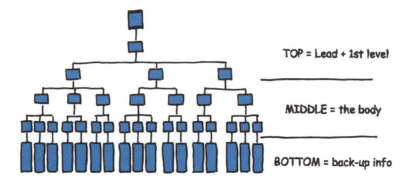

TOP = Lead + 1st level

MIDDLE = the body

BOTTOM = back-up info

Don't think that your work is finished. It happens almost never that you get a pyramid right first time. Now you need to adjust, switch things around, create new groups, etc. Keep on doing this until your pyramid is correct and fully meets all the requirements of the methodology.

Your aim is to develop a reasoning that your listeners will be able to understand with the lowest possible cognitive load. The way you group together your information in the pyramid has a crucial effect on this load. If you adhere to the following guidelines, you will note that your reasoning is clear for your audience, with the lowest possible mental effort.

Four ways to group your content

Your pyramid consists of different groups of assertions, each summarised by an overarching conclusion or summary statement. There are four different types of logic that can be used for this grouping process:

- deduction;
- induction;
- abduction;
- categories.

With **deductive reasoning**, one assertion or premise leads to another, forming a logical argument and leading, eventually, to a logical conclusion.

Example of deductive reasoning:

- The income of young artists is very irregular.
- Irregular income can lead to cash shortages at certain times.
- At such a time, the artist needs to take another job to make ends meet.
- This persuades many young artists to give up their art.
- This impoverishes the available choice of new art on the market.

Conclusion: the availability of new art on the market is becoming impoverished because the income of young artists is too irregular.

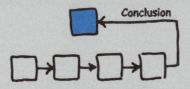

Deduction

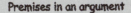

Premises in an argument

Deductive reasoning feels like the most 'intelligent' logic: it leads to a conclusion with mathematical certainty, provided that the premise is correct. But, even if many presenters prefer this reasoning, it does have a major drawback in terms of communication. It requires a high attention and cognitive effort to understand.

Inductive reasoning works differently. You base your conclusion on a list of separate arguments that support that conclusion. The arguments are not connected and do not follow on from each other, as is the case with deductive reasoning.

Example of inductive reasoning:

- Painters have an irregular income and often give up their art.
- Musicians have an irregular income and often give up their music.
- Sculptors have an irregular income and often give up their sculpting.

Conclusion: artists give up their art (probably) because they have an irregular income.

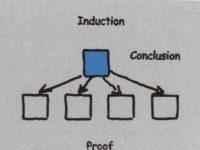

Induction

Conclusion

Proof

Note that inductive reasoning leads to a conclusion only with a certain degree of probability, whereas correct deduction leads to a conclusion with mathematical certainty. However, in terms of communication, induction is easier to understand, because it is a more natural way of thinking, with a lower cognitive load.

Abductive reasoning is very similar to inductive reasoning. It involves you starting with a certain statement and then going in search of its possible causes. This method is used often in research.

Example of abductive reasoning:

- Problem:
  - Many artists give up their art.
- Possible causes:
  - Their income is too irregular.
  - They do not enjoy the benefits of social security.
  - The price they get for their work is too low.
  - The market for their work is too small.

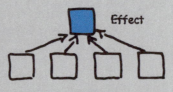

Abduction

Effect

Possible causes

Finally, there is the fourth method of grouping: **categories**. This is the simplest method and just groups the information into categories. Elements that have a common characteristic simply are put together in the same group, without a cause and effect.

Example of categorised reasoning:

- Artists earn their income in very different ways:
  - self-employed artist;
  - salaried artist;
  - part-time artist;
  - hobby artist.

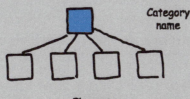

Category

Category name

Elements

It is simpler than other forms of logic, but doesn't really convey a message. It is therefore suitable only for the details of your presentation, but not for structuring important messages.

WHAT CRITERIA MUST YOUR PYRAMID SATISFY?

To check that your pyramid is perfect in both theoretical and practical terms, test it against the following six criteria:

1 There must be an overarching assertion (summary statement) at the top of each group.

2 Each group must contain elements of a similar kind.

3 The elements within a group must be in the right order.

4 Each group is exclusive and exhaustive.

5 Use the appropriate logic for each level.

6 The number of elements in each group is adjusted according to the level of abstraction.

If your pyramid satisfies these six criteria, your presentation will become a jewel of simplicity and you can move on with confidence to the next phase of your preparation. Here are the criteria in more detail:

1 There must be an overarching assertion at the top of each group

This overarching assertion must summarise succinctly all the underlying assertions or elements in the group. For a deductive or inductive group, the overarching assertion gives the conclusion drawn from all the elements in the group. In an abductive group, the assertion is the outcome of all the elements in the group. In a categorised group, the assertion is a generic term for all the elements in the group.

It should be obvious that, in these circumstances, a single word is less powerful and less communicative than a carefully worded statement. Your assertion should, therefore, contain at least one verb or adjective, but keep them reasonably short.

WEAK OVERARCHING ASSERTION	STRONG OVERARCHING ASSERTION
Sales figures	Sales are stable
Market share	We are losing market share
Project plan	The project will last for one year
In the commercial segment we have had stable results over the last two months. Brand XYZ has recovered from last year's dip and brand ABC experienced a (non-significant) fall	Results in the commercial segment are stable
We should remove questions that do not measure immediately what customers do, and only collect data that has a direct link with the behaviour of individual customers	We measure only behaviour of customers

Each group can, therefore, be read from top to bottom or bottom to top.

- **From top to bottom:** an assertion and a related question, with the different answers to that question underneath.
- **From bottom to top:** a number of statements/elements, with a summary above.

If you apply this logic consistently, the higher you go in the pyramid, the more abstract the assertions will be. And, the lower you go, the more concrete and detailed they will be. In a desperate attempt to find at least one sentence for their assertion, some presenters resort to 'empty' statements:

- 'There are seven things you must remember.'
- 'There are five possible solutions.'
- 'It is a four-step plan.'

Limit this trickery: empty assertions never carry a real message and therefore have less meaning.

2 Each group must contain elements of a similar kind

Put only related elements together in the same group. Things related to the production process should not be put in the same group with product characteristics. Think carefully about the different elements and make sure there is a logical reason for grouping them together.

Here is another example. It shows how poor grouping can be damaging for the understanding of your presentation. The first 'group' of elements clearly do not all belong together. As a result, all the 'arguments' are muddled and there is no logical coherence. The second group clearly does have more logic and coherence.

STEP 6
STRUCTURE

TITLE OUR NEW PRODUCT: HOME DELIVERY	TITLE HOME DELIVERY: RIGHT UP YOUR STREET!

• Deliveries every day throughout the country
 	
• Delivery cost: £10 for the customer, free for purchases over £150
 	
• All products can be delivered
 	
• Tests in urban environments were successful and led to a 15% increase in sales
 	
• Launch in January
 	
• The advertising campaign is being prepared
 	
• Three agencies have been invited to make a pitch
 	
• Investments in IT are budgeted
 	
• Limited effect on staff
	• Customers are interested:
	  – Daily deliveries
	  – Nationwide
	  – All products
	  – Low cost
	  – Successful in city tests
	
	• Good for business
	  – 15% extra sales
	  – IT costs are covered
	  – Low impact on staff
	
	• Ready for launch
	  – January = kick off!
	  – Advertising campaign is being prepared
	  – Three agencies are to pitch

3 The elements within each group must be in the right order

Arrange your arguments within the group in a logical order. This assists the memory and clarifies the logic of the grouping. The following small test illustrates this. Read the following list of words and try to memorise them.

universe – city – house – country – hill – stone – solar system – earth – village – continent

Most people who do this test manage to remember no more than 6 or 7 of the words after looking at them for 15 seconds. But what happens when you are presented with the list in the following manner?

stone – home – village – town – mountain – country – continent – earth – solar system – universe

In this case, about half the test subjects can remember all the words. Why? In the second list, the words are arranged in order of size. From small to big. The difference in size also emphasises this. The order you use in a grouping creates a relationship between the elements and implicitly reflects the reasoning you used when creating the group. It becomes easier to understand and remember. When choosing the order, try to put the most important element first (or last), because these are remembered most easily.

4 Each group is exclusive and exhaustive

Exclusive means that the elements of the group do not overlap. Exhaustive means that together they must contain all the information that is summarised in the statement above. The MECE (mutually exclusive and collectively exhaustive) principle was described in *The McKinsey Way* by Ethan Rasiel (Raisel, 1999) and also adopted by Barbara Minto. It helps you to think and communicate more clearly.

MECE   Not exclusive   Not exhaustive

When you group things according to the MECE principle, it is much easier for your listeners to understand.

Those crazy Belgians …

You can understand the MECE principle by looking at the organisation of the Belgian state. As a country, Belgium used to be divided into 10 provinces. The territory of each province is clearly defined: no province overlaps with any other province. Together, they form the country Belgium. Every Belgian knows in which province he resides. This applies equally for towns and municipal districts. Each municipal district also falls entirely within the boundaries of one of the provinces. There is no municipal district that overlaps the boundary between two provinces. These groups are therefore completely MECE.

Because of the regional and linguistic differences, Belgium is now also divided into three regions and three communities, each with its own government. This is a bit more complex. There are Walloons who speak French, Flemings who speak Dutch and the German speakers of the Eastern Cantons. Then there is the melting-pot of Brussels, the capital city, where French is mainly (but not exclusively) spoken. You would imagine that the Walloon region and the French-speaking community would coincide, but this is not the case. French-speaking is not equivalent to Walloon.

The German speakers also are part of the Walloon region, but are not part of the French-speaking community. And the people of Brussels have their own region, the Brussels Capital City Region, whose French-speaking inhabitants also belong to the French-speaking community, whilst its Dutch-speaking inhabitants belong to the Dutch-speaking community. But, even though the Dutch-speaking community has been fused with the Flemish region, the Dutch speakers in Brussels, whilst being members of the Dutch-speaking community, are **not** part of the Flemish region, since they live in the Brussels Capital City Region. **Are you still following? If not, don't worry!** Many Belgians don't understand it, either! But it does show how much more complex things are when they are not MECE.

5 Use the appropriate logic for each level

You have most freedom in the lower levels. Here you can arrange the information using any of the four grouping logics. In the middle level you must adhere strictly to the question-and-answer method using deductive, inductive or abductive logic. It is better to avoid categorisation, since this conveys little meaning. In the top level there is one more, and very important, limitation: here you must always use the inductive logic, never a deductive logic. Your presentation should never be one long reasoning. There are a number of reasons for this:

- Deduction requires greater mental effort from your audience.

- Deduction requires attention to be paid to each step of the reasoning; if you fail to understand a single step, you will fail to understand the reasoning as a whole.

- Likewise, if the audience questions one element of your deductive argument, the whole structure of your reasoning collapses. This is not the case with induction. Even if only four of your five arguments are valid, your conclusion remains valid as well (be it with a lower probability).

- Finally, deduction brings with it the temptation to keep the conclusion to the end. And, as we have already seen, in business presentations this is something you should never do.

6 The number of elements in each group is adjusted according to the level of abstraction

We create groups to overcome the limitations of our working memory. As you know now, the limit of the executive working memory is four to seven pieces of information. On top, abstract ideas are more difficult to process than concrete details. For this reason, I recommend using smaller groups near the top of your pyramid where information is important and abstract. You can use bigger groups the lower down you go. Having said that, groups that are too small should also be avoided, because they will make your pyramid unnecessarily high and your story unnecessarily long. Often you will see that the keynote of top speakers consists of a pyramid with just three elements in each group of the top two levels.

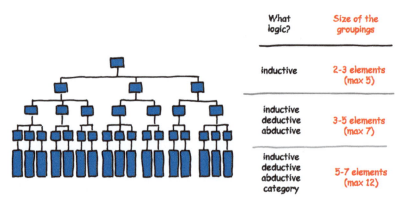

	What logic?	Size of the groupings
	inductive	2-3 elements (max 5)
	inductive deductive abductive	3-5 elements (max 7)
	inductive deductive abductive category	5-7 elements (max 12)

The upper levels of the pyramid require more attention to the groupings

WHAT ARE THE ADVANTAGES OF THE PYRAMID MODEL?

The pyramid model structures your information in a way that keeps the cognitive load as low as possible and is therefore easier to understand for your audience. But there are other practical advantages:

1 **You can shorten your presentation easily.** If you have constructed your pyramid properly, the most important ideas will be at the top and the detail will be at the bottom. You can shorten the presentation easily simply by drawing a horizontal line through the pyramid. Everything above the line will form a clear and coherent story. You have only five minutes? Then probably you will need to draw your line just under the highest level. You've got 10 minutes? Two levels should be enough. Half an hour? Three levels. And so on. You can keep the levels you don't use as back-up.

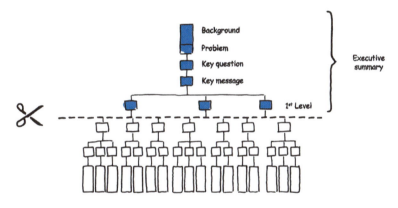

With a perfect pyramid structure
your presentation is shortened easily

2 **You have a number of different presentations in one.** You can use separate branches of your pyramid as separate presentations. The overarching assertion at the top of the branch is the key message for that particular sub-presentation.

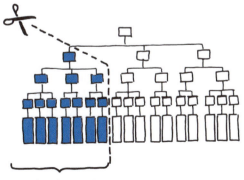

Partial presentation

STEP 6
STRUCTURE

3 **You have a ready-made conversation.** Because the pyramid has been built using a question-and-answer structure, it has the feel of a conversation. This gives a more natural impression. With a good pyramid, all the questions seem to come at the right moment: when the audience is ready for that question, you are there with the answer.

4 **Your reasoning is easy to follow.** You can approach every problem from a number of different angles. That is what many speakers do in their presentations. They jump from here to there and back again, because they want to deal with too many angles at the same time. When this happens, it is difficult for the audience to follow the reasoning. By focusing on one question, the pyramid method forces you to approach the problem in a simple manner, step by step, without changing your line of approach. As a result, it is easier to understand and remember.

5 **You maintain a good overview.** All your information is arranged neatly. The pyramid helps you, as a presenter, to remember the total picture. You have a clear overview of each moment. This will make you more confident and your presentation will be more fluent.

6 **You can build the pyramid with a group of people.** If you work in a team, all of you can work together on the same pyramid. This improves understanding and communication within the team.

7 **You save time.** Arranging ideas and information in the right order on paper is ten times quicker than using PowerPoint. Because first you reach an agreement about how everything will fit together, so you save a huge amount of time during the further development of your presentation.

IN SHORT

Now you have arranged all the knowledge and reasoning necessary for your presentation in a two-dimensional, pyramid-shaped structure. This will be your guide for the further preparation of your presentation, and during its actual delivery. Delete, refine and amend your map until it forms a beauty of logic and simplicity, obeying the rules of the pyramid principle:

1 There is an assertion or a proposition in each box, not just a word.

2 Working from top to bottom, the map reads like a question-and-answer conversation.

3 Working from bottom to top, each group of assertions forms one or more arguments that are summarised in an overarching assertion or conclusion.

4 At the highest level, only inductive logic is used.

5 All the groups of assertions are exclusive and exhaustive.

6 Each group of assertions is listed in a clear order, with the most important first.

PHASE 3
THE STORY

How do you make your presentation stick?

HANDLES – VISUAL – OUTLINE

Imagine that you represent an organisation that collects money for aid in Africa. You send out an email. You give lots of shocking statistics about how many people die from malaria, about the scarcity of health care and about the lack of proper education and prevention. You also list the number of projects you want to implement and give details of the necessary budgets. Finally, you ask your readers to give generously; after all, their money can save lives ... I put this scenario to 10 people of differing backgrounds and asked them how much money they would give. In each case, the answer was the same: 'Nothing!'. Why? Why do you think?

My son Henri has just completed his bachelor degree in medicine. During last year's summer holiday, he went with five of his fellow students to Uganda, travelling from village to village with local doctors and aid teams to provide basic medical help: vaccinations, consultations, distribution of medical supplies, information about HIV and other health education.

Henri sent a letter to family and friends, explaining his plans and asking them to sponsor his project. And what happened? Almost everyone gave him considerable support, often donating as much as £250 or more. People's generosity seemed to know no bounds.

What was the difference? Henri had a story to tell. A personal story. A story about someone they actually knew, not just some faceless organisation. What's more, he was planning to go himself and do something concrete, not just planning a vague theoretical program.

'Imagination is the power through which we gather knowledge.' Immanuel Kant

Up to now, you have concentrated on injecting your presentation with the necessary logic and simplicity. You have refined your material and arranged it in a logical manner. You have created a pyramid structure as a basis for your presentation. But the structure, important though it is, contains only logically ordered, naked information. It has objective value, but if this information needs to be brought to life with moving anecdotes, convincing images, sensory detail, personal insights and emotion ... Unless you can introduce these elements into your presentation, there is a risk that your listeners will not pay much attention to what you have to say and will not be touched by your message. You need to give your objective material a new subjective dimension: you need to give it a story dimension. Because it is only with a story that you can plant your key message deep in the memory of your audience.

How do you do this? By adding the following elements into your presentation mix:

1 Sensory handles that colour your ideas.
2 Images that help your audience to visualise your ideas.
3 A fluent storyline.

These three elements of subjective content will ensure that:

- you and your message both receive attention;
- you keep the attention throughout;
- your listeners understand the essence of your message better;
- they become emotionally engaged;
- new insights will remain fixed in the memory of your audience.

Last summer I visited my parents, who had guests from New Zealand. We were sitting in the garden on a sunny afternoon, when our guests were startled suddenly by something. At first, neither myself nor my parents could understand what had happened.

Our guests were from Christchurch. Some years earlier, their city had been hit by a terrible earthquake. The sounds and vibrations caused by a passing lorry vaguely resembled that of an earthquake and immediately set the alarm bells ringing inside their heads. Something that we hadn't even registered was enough to give them a really bad scare. Because their previous experience was such a traumatic one, the least sensory stimulation was sufficient to bring back this memory. It attracted their full attention, but none of ours.

How does attention work?

If you cannot attract the attention of your listeners, your key message will never become rooted in their minds. Getting and holding the attention of the audience is one of your most important tasks as a speaker.

At the beginning of a presentation, people's attention level is fairly high. But, before a quarter of an hour has passed, their attention reserves are already running low. You will need to work really hard to keep their attention for the full duration of a presentation. And you have more chance of being successful when you understand how attention works.

Our working memory needs to process hundreds of thousands of sensory inputs every day. They are all screaming for attention, but only a very few ever get it. The recognising memory analyses all incoming sensory input at lightning speed and decides which ones will be passed on to the executive memory.

Broadly speaking, we can distinguish three types of attention:

1 **Alerting attention.** This is what our New Zealand friends experienced. The passing lorry awakened the concept of earthquake in their minds and immediately alerted their attention. Everyone is programd to react in a particular way to particular sensory input. We have many of these programs in common, but some of them are also person-specific.

   You have probably experienced this for yourself. You are sitting in a bar, talking to a friend. There is a group at the next table, talking about this and that. You are not listening to their conversation, until you hear a single word that attracts your attention. Your own name! Your attention immediately springs into action ... And then you realise that you haven't heard the last sentence of what your friend said. Conclusion? Something rooted in your memory that has a strong emotional charge – like your own name – can attract your attention instantly and monopolise your cognitive resources.

   Use this knowledge in your presentation, by using things your listeners recognise:
   – Talk about concrete experiences that you know your listeners have had as well.
   – Use examples from the environment of your listeners.

- Use analogies and small details that have a connection with your listeners (are they dog-lovers, football fanatics, etc?).
- Use people's names when you are talking to them. If someone is not paying attention, just casually mention their name and watch what happens!

2 **Surprise attention.** Our brain gives special treatment to unusual things. In other words, unexpected things attract our attention. This works as follows. The incoming sensory input is compared with existing schemas in our long-term memory. When a corresponding schema is detected, the working memory limits itself to checking whether the incoming input continues to correspond with this schema, which requires less cognitive effort than fully analysing the input. But when, at a given moment, the memory discovers something that doesn't match, it immediately gets all our attention.

3 **Conscious attention.** Of course, we have the option to devote our attention deliberately to something. In this case, the executive working memory decides that something merits our attention. It then sends a request to the recognising memory to pass on the information or even to instruct our muscles to turn our head and eyes in the direction of the information.

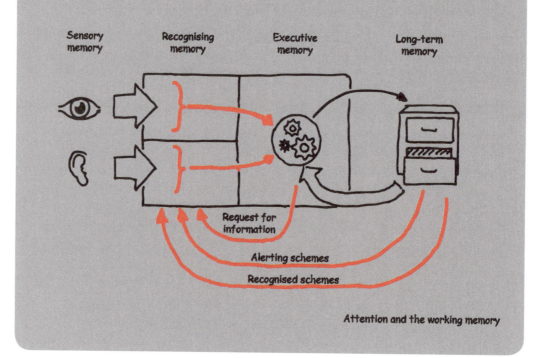

Attention and the working memory

STEP 7
Find your handles
Colour your message

At the time of writing this, I am sitting in Terminal F of Moscow Airport after a three-day workshop, waiting for my flight home. An elderly couple is dragging two large, old suitcases through the departure hall. These old models are impractical because they have just a single handle on the long side. The old man walks with a stoop, weighed down by the heavy load of the cases. A few steps later, he has to stop to help his wife, who can carry her massive case – it was almost bigger than her – no further.

Just behind them, a young family is also crossing the departure hall. Of course, they have modern suitcases, with extendable handles and wheels. The children are pulling their own cases behind them, and the parents also have a small travel bag on top of one of their cases.

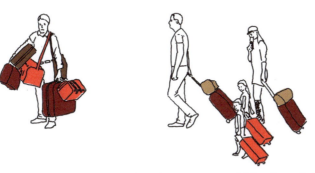

Provide your message with handles and wheels

Whilst I was watching, I was struck by the thought that those old suitcases were really awkward to use. All today's cases have wheels and three handles, which makes everything so much easier. These labour-saving models were invented only about 20 years ago by an American called

Don Ku. Ku was granted a patent for his idea in 1992, and his concept has totally changed the way we travel with luggage. Ku's case has a handle on the long side, so that you can carry it easily up the stairs to the departure lounge. But there is also one on the short side, so that you can manoeuvre it easily along the narrow aisle of a plane. Best of all, there is an extendable handle that allows you to pull the case on wheels over long distances. In other words, there is a handle suitable for every traveller and every situation.

The new knowledge that you want to communicate in your presentation is just like a suitcase. A huge suitcase packed with information that your listeners need to carry deep into their memory. Without the right handles they will not be able to move it very far. So you need to do what Don Ku did: provide your presentation with handles and wheels, in the shape of sensory and narrative elements that will allow your listeners to carry your message with ease and roll it confidently into the deepest recesses of their memory.

Handles ensure that your message penetrates the working memory and then sticks permanently in the long-term memory of your audience. How many handles do you need? That depends on both your subject and your audience: the more diverse your audience and the less they know about the subject, the more handles you need to offer them.

There are three ways in which a handle makes your message more memorable:

1 It attracts people's attention.
2 It makes your message clearer.
3 It makes your message easier to remember.

What makes a good handle? There are plenty of options:

- images;
- examples;
- anecdotal stories;
- analogies and metaphors;
- surprise elements;
- emotions;
- quotations;
- experience and experiments;
- questions;
- humour;
- figures and percentages.

We will look at each of these individually. Images are so important that I devote a complete chapter to them.

Sensory integration and elaborate encoding

Our working memory does not treat the input from our senses separately. Rather, it combines the input from different senses to give meaning. This is called sensory integration and it is essential for us to understand what happens around us. Remember the McGurk Effect (page 70) that proves how visual and auditory inputs are combined.

Moreover, the more sensory input that is available at the moment of learning, the stronger the memory of that learning will be. If I told you that my friend Graham likes motorbikes, probably you would forget about him very quickly. But, if I told you so when you met him in his garage, amidst his race bikes, felt his strong handshake, smelled the oil and burned tires, saw him wearing his race overalls with the worn knee pads, and experienced his megawatt smile when he talked about the latest track day, you'd probably never forget him. That is called elaborate encoding and it is a way to help your audience integrate the new knowledge and remember it.

Co-authors and speakers Dan and Chip Heath have explained this mechanism by comparing our memory with Velcro: on one side, velcro has thousands of little eyes; the other side has thousands of little hooks (Heath and Heath, 2007). If you push both sides firmly against each other, the hooks fit neatly into the eyes, so that both sides stick together. Your memory works in just the same way. Your brain is one side: the side with thousands of little eyes. This is where you want to 'stick' a memory. To do this, you need a story with as many small hooks as possible. Each hook is a sensory detail. And the more these hooks contain new information, the better they will be able to latch on to the eyes. So, don't tell stories about 'the average worker'; instead tell stories about an individual. About Robert, for example. He has worked for 23 years on the assembly line. With the passage of time he has lost some hair and gained some kilos, but he is still as motivated as ever; someone who is proud of never being late, and sets a great example for the youngsters ... This is the kind of person you need in your stories.

GIVE EXAMPLES

We all know that a good example speaks volumes. Examples make abstract ideas more tangible in the mind of your audience. They make things clear and understandable, and help to simplify otherwise complex reasonings. Imagine that your key message is 'our customer friendliness is getting worse'. You can illustrate this with concrete examples: 'Last month we had 239 complaints from customers. Take Gerry, for example. Last week he wrote as follows ...' And then you read out Gerry's letter. Show the pile of other letters of complaint and you will underline your point even further.

TELL (SHORT) STORIES

Originally coming from the town of Ypres, my most vivid knowledge of the Great War doesn't come from history books, but from stories I was told by old inhabitants or by the family of fallen British soldiers who visit the town.

Stories have always been popular. From the dawn of human history, people have been telling each other stories and parables, whether they are about the Great War, Moses, Buddha or King Arthur. Values have been communicated from generation to generation through narrative tales.

'A story is a re-imagined experience narrated with enough detail and feeling to cause your listeners' imaginations to experience it as real.' Annette Simmons

Our brains are made to listen to and interpret stories. Oral culture existed long before mankind learnt to read and write, so our brains are wired to understand and remember stories. Stories have the power to fix information more firmly in the memory.

Where can you find stories? Just look around you! The more closely your story relates to reality, the better. Using the ideas of Annette Simmons from her book *Whoever Tells the Best Story Wins* (Simmons, 2007), I have drawn up the following list as a source of inspiration:

- **Personal stories** based on your own experience.
  - **Who am I stories.** Who am I, what drives me?
  - **Why am I here stories.** Why am I giving this presentation?
  - **Learning stories.** Stories that you, personally, have learnt from: successes, failures, what you have learnt from your mentor(s).
- **Business stories** from your professional environment.
  - **Value stories.** How a value exists in your company: 'John, one of our drivers, is fanatical about punctuality because ...'
  - **Vision stories.** Your company's vision in your own words: 'I dream that one day our company will ...'
  - **Competition stories.** What successes have your competitors realised? What were their failures? What are they doing now? What can you learn from them?
  - **Customer stories.** Tell the real-life stories of a customer.
  - **Comparison stories.** About other departments or other companies: How do they do this at Apple? Or at Lu? How did Microsoft get so big and Coca-Cola so strong?
  - **Research stories.** Link your presentation to scientific research results.
- **Stories about your audience.** This increases their involvement even more.
  - **What does your audience think?** Put yourself in their shoes. Say what you would do in their place: 'Now, you probably think that ...'
  - **Success stories.** About someone in the room: 'So Bob has managed to increase sales in his sector by an amazing 35 per cent, thanks to ...'
  - **Opposition stories.** Neutralise possible negative comments by offering them as your own thoughts – and refuting them: 'A financial expert probably will ask himself why ...'
- **Famous stories**
  - Just like children, we love to listen to stories we are familiar with, especially the powerful ones.

It is always a good idea to try out your stories first on someone else. Do they work? Are they suitable for the message you want to give? Watch for the reaction of your audience during the presentation. If your stories don't set the audience alight, you will know how to do it differently next time.

The episodic memory

In Part I we focused on the working memory. We distinguished three separate components: the visual and auditory recognising memories and the executive memory. In 2000 Baddeley added a fourth element: the episodic buffer or, as I call it, the episodic memory (Baddeley, 2000). The episodic memory retains information in chronological order. Literally 'chrono-logical': in a logical, time-related order. It seems that we can remember experiences better in this manner.

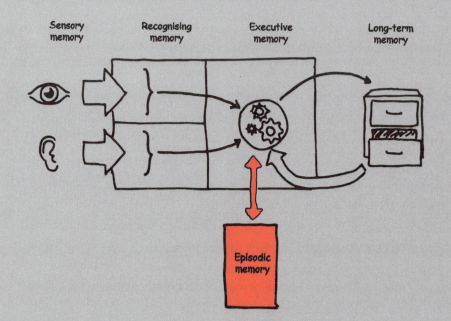

We have a separate memory for stories

Information that is fed to the working memory in the form of a chronological sequence of events can be stored easily in the episodic memory and just as easily recalled from there. In other words, if you give information in the form of a story, you can partly get around the storage limitations of the working memory. The episodic memory also has a direct link to the long-term memory, helping us to remember stories over a longer period.

This explains why stories are such an important means of communication. The more information you can give in story-form, the more easily it will be remembered.

USE ANALOGIES AND METAPHORS

Do you know what a Can-Am Spyder Roadster is? If you do, play the sport, and pretend you have never heard of it.

A Can-Am Spyder Roadster is a motorised vehicle made by the Bombardier Company. It has two wheels at the front with an independent suspension and a single rear-drive wheel. The engine is placed centrally, just behind the front wheels. You steer the vehicle with a horizontal steering bar that turns on a vertical axle and on which accelerator and brake handles are also mounted. The driver sits in the middle, just in front of the back wheel, and there is room for one passenger behind him. Neither the driver nor the passenger are protected against wind and rain; only a small windshield provides minimal protection. The vehicle has a steel frame and plastic bodywork.

Try to picture this vehicle in your mind. It's not easy, is it? But, what if I say:

'A Can-Am Spyder Roadster is a snow scooter on wheels.'

With far fewer words you get a much better picture of what a Can-Am really is. You need recall only the image of a snow scooter from your long-term memory and replace the skis and the caterpillar track with wheels.

The first description required 115 words – and even then it is difficult to visualise what the vehicle looks like. The second description – an analogy – took just nine words, but you could see immediately a Can-Am in your mind's eye.

Analogies and metaphors are powerful communication enhancers. Their power lies in the fact that they make use of information already stored in your long-term memory. Instead of explaining a subject in great detail, you compare it with something else that your listeners are familiar with. With a little information you have created a new knowledge that is fixed far more firmly in the memory of your listeners and with far less mental effort.

Metaphors generally are shorter than analogies and don't make such an elaborate comparison between the two things, and convey a more emotional concept.

A nice example was a CEO of a producer of detergents who finished his international sales conference with one picture. In a photo of New Zealand's All Blacks, performing their impressive Haka, he had replaced the faces of the players with managers in his company. All the opponents, who watched the All Blacks in fear, had the logos of the competitors on their shirts. The picture needed no words.

SURPRISE!

A while ago, I was on a flight coming back from Singapore. As is usual just before take-off, one of the flight stewards moved forward to give the standard talk about safety precautions. He began as follows: 'Good morning, ladies and gentlemen. Please note that you will be permitted to smoke during this flight.' … Short silence … Everyone looked up in surprise. 'But only on our sun terrace, which you will find on the first floor, where you have a fantastic view. Unfortunately, it's a little windy up there, and the temperature can drop to –50° Celsius. So, make sure you wrap up nice and warm.' After that he continued with the usual safety demonstration. But, in the meantime, his unexpected introduction had captured everyone's attention – and the plane was full of smiling people.

It is built into our genes. Whenever something unexpected happens, our senses switch to alarm mode. We become much more focused – no doubt a throw-back to the days when we lived in caves and needed to be on our guard against all kinds of hidden dangers.

Tips for the use of surprise effects

1 Make sure that your surprises are not pre-dictable but are post-dictable. People shouldn't be able to see your surprises coming, but they must be able to understand them afterwards, so that they can see how the surprise is linked to your theme.

2 Use the element of surprise at the right moment. For example, just before you are going to say something important. Because that's when you want the audience to be alert.

3 Don't confuse a surprise with a gimmick. More often than not, gimmicks work against you. You can begin your presentation by singing a song but, unless your subsequent content is iron-strong, all the audience will remember are your false notes and bad tone!

You can also use surprise to make an overconfident audience think again. Recently I gave a presentation to a group of marketing specialists. They had been in the sector for years and thought they knew it all. It is very hard to bring new insights to this kind of audience unless you can snap them out of their hubris with a surprise.

I asked: 'Do you know something about figures?' A few of them nodded in a manner that suggested 'of course we do'. The others didn't even bother to reply. 'OK,' I said. 'There are 38 of us in this room. What is the likelihood that two people have the same birthday?' This was not what they had been expecting: I had their attention. I let them think about it for a while and then asked a few of them to tell me their answer: '6 per cent', '0.7 per cent', '9.4 per cent'. No one gave an answer that was higher than 11 per cent. The majority thought that there was a less than 1 per cent chance.

'Well, the chance is actually … 89.9 per cent.' Now they were all wide awake! 'How could we possibly be so wide of the mark?' I explained the maths and we did the test – and indeed, discovered that two of the participants did have the same birthday: 28 August. Now everyone understood that they still had something to learn and gave their full and undivided attention to my speed course in marketing statistics.

PLAY WITH EMOTIONS

If used wisely, emotions sharpen the attention, stimulate the memory and give people a greater sense of involvement. Encouraging strong emotions in your audience works well. Positive, and even negative, emotions ensure that the audience remembers your presentation better than otherwise would be the case.

We remember something better if it has a strong emotion attached to it

Research has shown how emotion influences our cognitive memory (Brosch 2013 and Kensinger, 2009): it increases our attention at the moment of encoding. It also increases the consolidation of the memory and facilitates its recollection.

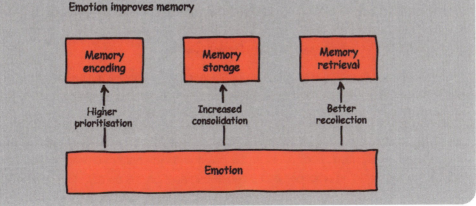

Emotion improves memory

This is something that happens all the time in police work at crime scenes. When there is a gun involved, people seem to remember only the gun, because that is the most frightening thing. All the other details (how many robbers there were, what the colour of the car was, etc.) are not stored or recollected in as much detail when a gun is involved.

Kensinger measured the strength of encoding memories using functional magnetic resonance imaging (fMRI): when an emotion is involved, the signal is much stronger. And it is stronger for a negative emotion than for a positive emotion.

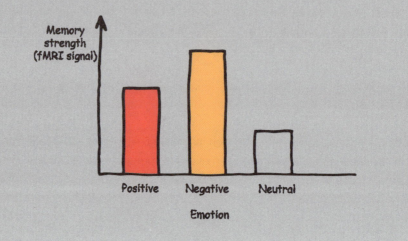

Emotions also influence our decisions. Positive emotions will make it easier for people to agree with you. If you want to obtain a positive decision, try to make sure that your listeners are nodding in approval throughout your presentation. Once they get into the 'yes' mood, the chance is much greater that they will actually go along with the proposed decision at the end of the presentation.

Negative emotions will make it less likely that people go along with your proposal. Even when people are convinced of the logic of an argument, they will sometimes choose a different option, or refuse to decide for purely (negative) emotional reasons.

For this reason, you need to be careful about how you use negative emotions in your presentation:

- **Allow (negative) emotions in your presentation.** It is certainly ill-advised to try and eliminate negative emotions. Give people the chance to express what they feel. It is much worse to sweep a difficult subject under the carpet than to confront it head on. Research has shown that suppressing emotions has a negative impact on the quality of decision making.

- **Name the emotions.** Emotions are easier to deal with if they have been recognised and named. Named emotions have more positive and less negative effects.

- **Prepare the way for negative emotions.** If you are about to tackle a sensitive subject, it is best to prepare your audience. Tell them in advance that it might feel uncomfortable. Patrick Lencioni, best-selling author of *The Five Dysfunctions of a Team*, calls this 'real time permission', meaning it is better to announce a conflict rather than just waiting for it to happen (Lencioni, 2002).

'Ladies and gentlemen. Today we are taking the decision to close down a project in which we have invested £100,000. This fills us with sadness, because we experience this decision as a defeat. Perhaps some of you are angry at the money wasted ...'

Emotions and decisions

In the **Ultimatum Game**, used in neuro-economic experiments, a player is given a certain sum of money; for example, £20. This player – player A – must share this money with another player – player B. The way he shares the money is up to player A. He can split it equally with player B, £12–£8, £14–£6, £16–£4, etc. Or, he can decide to keep it all for himself. Player B has the right to accept or reject the offer. If he rejects it, both players end up with nothing. Logically speaking, a player who thinks rationally should accept any offer of £1 or more. He had nothing; if he accepts, he will at least have something. But tests carried out around the world reveal a very different picture. Players nearly always reject an offer of less than £5 because they consider it to be 'unfair'. In other words, emotion triumphs over reason.

- This illustrates how we combine emotion and reason when making decisions:
  - First reaction (reason): I am happy with £1 (better than nothing).
  - Second reaction (emotion): it is unfair, I want half (£10).
  - Third reaction (emotional control): £5 is reasonable, it's in between.

But bringing emotional and rational arguments in balance requires a serious cognitive effort, especially if the emotion is a negative one. This is another reason to keep the cognitive load of your presentation to a minimum. It allows your audience extra room to regulate their own emotions, which in turn will lead to better decisions. So, if negative emotions are involved, keep your messaging really simple.

Attempting to avoid the emotion is worst. Studies have also shown that suppressing emotions leads to a higher cognitive load and worse decisions. This again argues in favour of encouraging the display of emotions and making them discussable.

Heilman proved this theory in 2010 with the following experiment (Heilman & Liviu, 2010). He measured the quality of decisions made by students who had just been told their examination results. Some students were disappointed. They had expected to do better. Others were delighted, because they had passed with flying colours. Heilman asked some of the students to control their emotions (the reappraisers) by re-evaluating the meaning and importance of the situation. He asked the other group consciously to show no emotion whatsoever (the suppressors). A control group was asked to give its emotions free rein. Next, all the students were required to take a number of decisions that involved a certain degree of uncertainty and risk evaluation. Heilman measured the quality of their decisions.

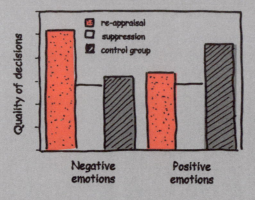

The way of dealing with emotion impacts the quality of decisions

What transpired? The quality of the decision making was always lower when emotions were suppressed. Reappraisal consistently led to better results when negative emotions were involved.

Emotion at the Stock Exchange

Mark Fenton-O'Creevy investigated the impact of emotion on the decisions taken by traders on the London Stock Exchange. His research showed that emotions and their control had an important impact on the quality of the decisions (Fenton-O'Creevy et al., 2010).

The results showed differences between high- and low-performance traders. Both categories deal differently with emotion and intuition. They opt for different emotional control strategies.

Traders who adopt a predictive emotional control strategy (which 'foresees' the emotions) perform better than those who adopt a responsive strategy (which reacts to emotions when they occur). This is yet another good reason for 'announcing' emotions in advance during your presentation: 'Ladies and gentlemen, none of us will enjoy this. The decision we need to take will hurt us all deeply. But, if we can set our disappointment to one side and look at the situation dispassionately, then we will see that this is the only possible solution.'

SPRINKLE YOUR PRESENTATION WITH QUOTES

Quotations have proved their value in presentations time and time again. Good quotes stick in the memory. So don't try to reinvent the wheel. Make use of what others have said before you.

Quotations increase your credibility. They make use of one of the six influencing methods described by Robert Cialdini in his book *Influence: Science and Practice*: authority (Cialdni, 2000). When someone with authority says something, we are more inclined to believe it.

But, when you take quotations from the internet, make sure you check their accuracy. I once made a big mistake. During a presentation I attributed a particular quote to Anton Chekov: 'I am writing a long letter because I don't have time to write a short one.' Until someone in the hall put up his hand and informed the whole room that these were not words of the Russian writer, but the French mathematician and philosopher Blaise Pascal. Talk about a red face! There are numerous good quotation sites on the web. There is also a selection on my site **www.edgruwez.com**.

INVOLVE THEM WITH ACTION

I once did a little experiment with the management team of a supermarket chain. The subject of the presentation was how the customer friendliness of the checkout staff could be improved. During the presentation, I made use of an actor to play the role of a customer. I asked the managers one by one to take place behind a (fictive) till and imagine they were a cashier.

To begin with, these top managers were surprised and embarrassed. But they quickly got in to their temporary role. And the experiment worked really well. By the end of the meeting, the managers understood how difficult it is for cashiers to remain friendly in all situations.

This experiment made clear to me how effective it is to involve people actively during your presentation. It strengthens the impact of your message. Everything they do in this 'hands-on' manner is more easily remembered. There is so much energy involved in personal experience that it still surprises me that speakers don't make more use of it.

'I hear and I forget. I see and I remember. I do and I understand.' Confucius

Once again, you need to be careful that you don't go to extremes. During one presentation I witnessed how the audience were asked to give their left shoe to their neighbour. They were not very impressed ...

GET THEM THINKING

Getting your audience involved doesn't always have to mean physical involvement. The most obvious way is to ask them questions. Pose your question and let them think about it, individually or in group, before giving an answer. Thinking about something activates the working memory. Asking questions gives your presentation a more natural, conversational feel, whilst at the same time increasing levels of attention.

GET THEM LAUGHING

In the film Django Unchained *by Quentin Tarantino, a group of white racists gang together to terrorise their black neighbours. All of them have pulled on the notorious KKK disguise to preserve their anonymity. It is a tragic episode from mankind's history set to film. Until the group starts to discuss their pointy hoods. They are uncomfortable, itchy and make it hard to see! The result is a scene that is both funny and pathetic: the 'tough' white man made to look foolish and scared.*

Humour acts as a wake-up call to our minds, stimulating our brain cells, putting us in a good mood and allowing us to see things in another perspective.

Having said this, using humour is not easy. A bad joke can boomerang in your face, often doing more harm than good. But that is no reason for not trying. Because, if you can get your audience laughing, you will score lots of points. And, if you don't feel comfortable telling a joke, why not use a cartoon:

Don't explain a joke. Wait and see if the audience reacts. If they don't, just move on to your next point (and make a mental note to scrap the joke from your next presentation). As always, make sure there is a link between your joke and your subject. If the joke then doesn't work, you can pass it off as an illustrative example, not intended for laughter.

FIGURES AND PERCENTAGES

Obviously, a presentation packed with figures, graphics and statistics should be avoided at all costs. Figures have a powerful effect if they are used sparingly as a handle.

A shocking figure can quickly capture people's attention. You can even strengthen the effect first by asking the audience to guess the answer to a question: 'What percentage of smartphone users admit that they can't do without their smartphone for more than an hour a day?' Pause here for greater impact. 'The answer is 65 per cent! And a quarter of users say that they never leave their phone out of reach ...'

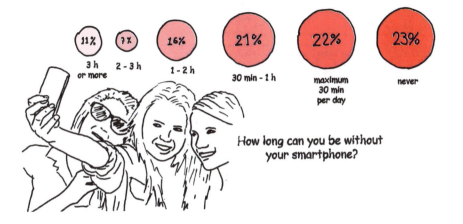

Percentages often mean more to people than figures. They are often smaller (maximum 100) and everyone can see the proportions.

> '15 per cent of our expenditure is spent on advertising. Whilst just 0.75 per cent is spent on competence development. That's 20 times less!'

Of course, the opposite sometimes is true. The statement that 'There are still 880,000 slaves in the European Union' is more powerful than '0.17 per cent of the European Union's total population are still slaves.'

PUT HANDLES IN STRATEGIC PLACES

You need to add your various handles at strategic places in the pyramid structure you made earlier, so that they attract attention and illustrate your message at key moments.

But be careful how many you use and where you put them. Don't use a new photo with every new slide. It is better to use one strong image that you can refer to consistently. Focus on the important concepts and messages you want your audience to remember.

How do you add handles to your pyramid structure? Think and work in a practical manner:

- Note down your handles on a Post-it® Note and stick them onto your pyramid where you think they will do most good. If you see later that they can be used better elsewhere, just move them.
- Or just write them into your pyramid in pencil (if you have made it on paper).

Spread your handles throughout the entire presentation, so that the attention of your audience is 'refreshed' at regular intervals. A new handle every 10 to 15 minutes is about right.

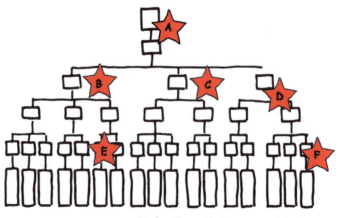

Six handles added to a pyramid structure

IN SHORT

After this phase of your preparation, you have the handles you need to attract and keep the attention of your audience. You have placed them in your pyramid structure at regular intervals. As handles come in all shapes and sizes, you have used a variety of different kinds to build the surprise effect into your presentation.

Remember that the handles must have a clear link with your subject. Think carefully about the effect you are trying to create. This must be positive.

STEP 7
HANDLES

STEP 8
Visualise your message
Use 'sticky' images

In the British film The Perfect Sense, *Ewan McGregor plays a young chef who falls in love with a scientist. At the same time, the world is in the grip of a strange epidemic, which causes people to lose their senses, one by one.*

People first lose their sense of smell and then their sense of taste. This is a nightmare for all, but life goes on and people adjust to the new situation. Until, in the end, they also go blind. They were still able to cope without the other senses, but without the sense of sight the world grinds to a halt.

Our sight is probably the most important of all our senses. The McGurk Effect (page 70) proves that sight overrides our hearing when signals are incoherent. Another example is the Can-Am Spyder (in the previous chapter): it is much easier to 'understand' an image than a complex explanation. Images also make it easier to remember things. This is confirmed by a number of scientific facts (Mayer, 2009):

- People remember words better when they are accompanied by an image.
- People understand concepts better if they are represented visually.
- People remember images longer than speech or the written word.

Images activate the memory

Is this true? Let's find out. The following list of words consists of two words that are not normally associated with each other. Read the full list just once. Then cover the right-hand side of the list. Wait 15 seconds and then see how many of the covered words you can remember.

car	–	terrace
town	–	flower
bus	–	tree
leopard	–	board
chair	–	bike
child	–	tractor
rain cloud	–	house
spider	–	hearth

How did you do? I have done this test with lots of people (albeit in a slightly different setting) and their average score was a lowly 1.7 words out of 8.

Now look at the full list again. This time form a visual image in your mind that brings the two words together. For example, a child sitting on a tractor. Now do the test again. Better? In my tests, people now scored an average of 7.7 words from 8. This is simply because you can now 'see' the information visually. Admittedly, in this test we created an image in our mind's eye. But the same effect can be created in your presentation by showing real images.

Numerous research studies have confirmed that sight is our most important sense. Graphics and visuals have a positive effect. They allow us to understand things more easily, convince us better and increase our ability to remember. In addition, they encourage us to have a positive attitude (Rossiter & Percy, 1980).

Research by Mayer revealed that the average results of students improved significantly when the material to be learnt was presented visually rather than in text form (Mayer, 2009). In fact, the improvement effect size was 1.4 (the effect size is the difference in score with and without images, divided by the standard deviation):

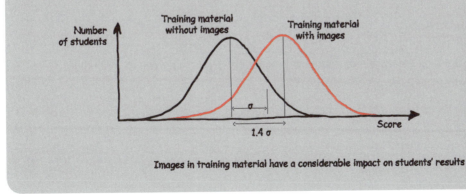

Images in training material have a considerable impact on students' results

Images improve our decision making

Which of the following statements is correct?

1 The daughter of the uncle of my father is the granddaughter of my great-grandfather.

2 The daughter of the uncle of my father is the granddaughter of the brother of my grandfather.

Admit it, you don't have an immediate answer, do you? But, if you are given a family tree to help you, things suddenly become much clearer:

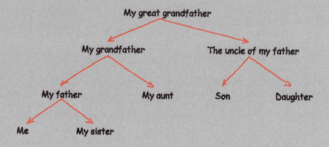

Presenting complex information in a visual way is a particularly good idea when there are a large number of relationships between the different elements contained in the information. The visual representation reduces the cognitive load.

Research by Bensabat and Dexter (1985) also illustrates how data presented as graphics (and not in tables) has a positive influence on the speed and quality of decision making.

BE SELECTIVE

Many managers are tempted to cram their presentations full of images. Unfortunately, it's not quite as easy as that.

If you add images to your presentation that are relevant, then obviously you are on the right track. But it is not a good idea per se to add a new image on each slide. You must refrain from making too much use of images simply to 'tart up' your slides. This simply produces additional cognitive load without benefit.

What's more, if the images have no relevance to your subject, they can even be harmful. So use images only if they have a clear added value and use them sparingly, so they can have maximum effect.

WHICH VISUALS SHOULD YOU CHOOSE?

You can divide visuals into two broad groups. On the one hand, you have figures and diagrams; on the other hand, you have photographs. Figures and diagrams can also be further subdivided into different categories.

Figures and diagrams

- **Spatial-visual figures,** such as maps, molecules and atoms, drawings.
- **Abstract representations,** such as organograms, Venn diagrams, family trees, etc. These figures have no real spatial-visual meaning, but we use them as a kind of visual metaphor for abstract concepts.
- **Pictorial elements** depict things in a more or less visual manner.
- **Graphics** make numerical information visible.
- **Visual metonymy** is a method to call up an idea with a visual of something else associated with it. A typical example is the famous 'thumbs-up' in Facebook for 'I like'.

INSPIRATION FOR ABSTRACT REPRESENTATIONS

Use the following sketches as a source of inspiration for your visual representations.

Choices and decision

Choice

Decision

Decision

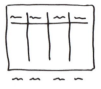
Evaluate multiple choices

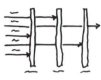
Decision tree

Evaluate multiple choices

Status and measurement

Measure

Measure - size

Measure - state

Measure - speed

State - less / more

State: full / empty

Hidden (problems)

Equilibrium

Resistance

Opposition

Tension

Networks and structures

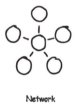
Network

Network

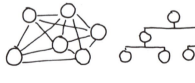
Network

Hierarchy

Parts of a whole

Overlap

Appropriate parts

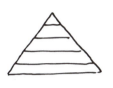

Pyramidal subdivision

Matrix subdivision

Subdivision

Hierarchical subdivisions

Parts of a whole

Parts of a whole

Problems

Problem

Problem

Blockage

Blockage

Temporary blockage

Problem

Problem

Danger

Solutions

Solution

Solution

Solution

Solution - exit

Green light

Idea - solution

Solution

Processes

Process (simple)

Process steps

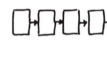

Process - steps

Subprocesses

Intermediate stages

Sub-steps

Selection

From - to

Converging

Converging

Diverging

Diverging

Circular processes

Circular process

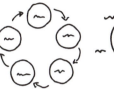
Circular stages

Circular process

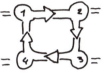
Circular process

Loop

Increase and decrease

Increasing

More and more

More and more

Decreasing

Less and less

Less and less

HOW DO YOU USE PHOTOS?

'People learn better from words and pictures than from words alone.' Richard Mayer

Why should you use photos in your presentation? The answer is simple: to increase and improve its sensory quality. The images you use must simplify, support and emphasise your

STEP 8
VISUAL

key message. For example, they might recall a mental image of real customers. Or reflect an emotion you want to stimulate.

For very simple slides you might risk adding a decorative visual element. But be careful that this does not overshadow the slide's message. If a slide already contains a lot of information, don't do it. People will focus too much on the image and not enough on the information.

Sometimes you can use images to influence subtly the thinking of your audience. You can do this by a technique known as 'framing'. This involves the use of an image to influence implicitly the frame of reference that your audience uses to interpret the message. The following slides use different photos with the same message. See what the pictures do with the message:

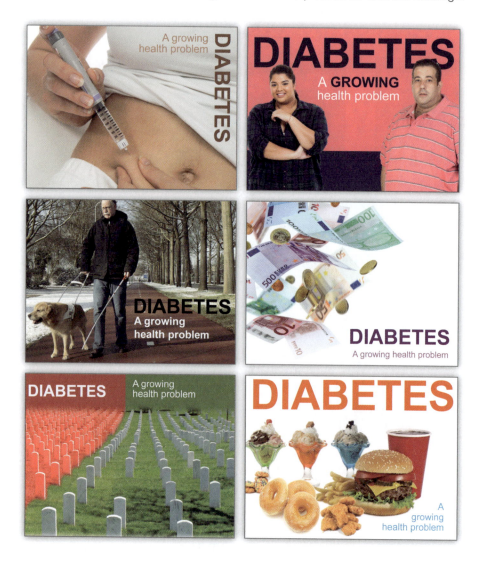

WHERE CAN YOU FIND YOUR PHOTOS?

Make use of a photobank with so-called 'stock pictures'. Usually they are not expensive and, in many cases, are even free. The latter often are of a poorer quality, but still good enough for many presentations. If you pick photos from the internet, make sure that they are rights-free. For links to photobank sites, visit **www.edgruwez.com**.

IN SHORT

In this step you have supported your key message with a number of key visuals. You allow these to recur regularly throughout the presentation.

Photos are useful for arousing emotions. They are both realistic and moving. Figures and diagrams bring clarity. They illustrate and enhance.

STEP 9

Sketch your outline

Find a natural flow

We once organised a two-day international marketing conference for one of our clients, a large pharmaceutical company. There were numerous international speakers, sharing the latest marketing insights in the pharmaceutical world. And, as the overall organiser, we asked for feedback from the participants at the end of the event. But, instead of asking for the usual evaluation of each speaker, we asked the speakers what the key message was and we asked the participants to tell us what they had learnt. You've guessed it! The results were not so good. Less than half of the participants could remember the key message of more than half the speakers. Seventy-five per cent of all key messages were lost. And we noticed that all the key messages that were remembered came from the same speakers. What was so different about this group? They were not the most flamboyant speakers, but they were the ones who clearly had a structured story that was easy to follow.

'No one pays attention to a boring story.' John Medina

The time has come now to write the storyline for your presentation. Lots of things have been said and written about how to write a storyline. But, if you have done all the right things during the previous phases of your preparation, writing out your story should be relatively easy now:

- Your introduction – or 'lead' – is more or less ready.
- The rest of your content is structured in the pyramid structure. Now you need to work this two-dimensional structure into a story by putting all your assertions in a sequential order.
- You have a number of handles – narrative and illustrative elements – to give your story colour.
- You have fixed your setting, so you know how you want to interact with your audience.

Now all you need to do is put it all together in the right order, using the right bridges that will allow you to move easily from one subject to another. Your story must be as clear as possible, so that people know, at any given moment, where you are in your presentation. And, of course, when you get to the end, you need to round up and make sure that you achieve your objective.

WRITE YOUR STORY STEP BY STEP

When I say it is time to write your story, I do not mean that you need to set down every word on paper. Instead, you should make a kind of scenario; the 'red thread' that you want to follow through the presentation, from your opening words to your final conclusion. And, as with any story, there are three parts: the beginning, the middle and the end.

The beginning: a good introduction

Your introduction is always based on the 'lead' that you have already written to 'hook' your audience at the start of the presentation. This lead consists of three or four elements: the situation, the complication (and key question), and your key message.

To get your audience's full attention, generally it is a good idea to start off first with a handle. Use an anecdote or give an example that emphasises the key complication.

> 'Ladies and gentlemen, I want to tell you about something that happened to me three years ago, before I started working for this company. After I moved house, I wanted to change my bank. So, I asked a number of friends and acquaintances who work in a bank – six, to be precise – to tell me why their bank would be best for me. What do you think they told me? Five of the six actually said: "Ed, you are better off going somewhere else." Can you believe that? They were unwilling to recommend their own bank! This truly happened. Can you guarantee that our staff wouldn't say the same about our company?'

The reason for giving this presentation is the potential complication you have detected: a possible lack of brand engagement amongst staff. The situation is the summary of everything you and they already know about current levels of engagement. The key question is implicitly present, but can also be projected explicitly on the screen: 'How can we make every member of staff a walking advertisement for our company?' This sounds much better than a title full of jargon: 'Brand engagement: analysis, monitoring and strategy'.

Do you always use the situation, complication and solution in that same order in your introduction? No. Changing the order will give your presentation a different emotional load.

Let me illustrate this by looking again at the example of Step 5 about the reorganisation of the supermarket chain:

- **Situation:**
  - During the last 10 years the number of products and commercial actions has risen dramatically, whilst the organisation has remained the same.
  - The store managers increasingly are unhappy; many are suffering from burn-out.
  - There are different possible explanations for this.
  - An independent study has been made.
- **Complication:**
  - We have reached the point where action is needed.
  - Key question: What do we need to change?
- **Solution (key message):**
  - Reduce the workload of store managers by redistributing some of their responsibilities.

Imagine this presentation needs to be given to three different target groups:

1 **The management committee:** who have to make the decision. They want no messing about and expect you to come straight to the point.

2 **The store managers:** who will be affected by the change. They need to support the change proposal, so this will require a little more empathy. You must show that you understand their position and want to do something about it.

3 **An award-jury:** For them, you need to make a clear and logical analysis of the case and all its effects.

Each of these presentations will require a different ordering of your introduction.

1 **Start with the key message for the management committee:** 'Ladies and gentlemen, I stand here before you with a proposal that will thoroughly transform the job content of your store managers.' After this, you can explain why the transformation is necessary: the situation and the complication that can no longer be avoided. This is as direct as it gets. You have outlined the key message in your opening sentence. There is no point beating about the bush. Your attitude is direct, to the point, business-like.

2 **Start with the complication for the store managers:** 'Ladies and gentlemen, things cannot carry on like this any longer. We have reached the point where it is impossible for you to do everything that the company expects. Your work pressure has passed the point that is reasonable.' Here you begin with the complication, which you throw out immediately to anchor their attention. First you show that you are here to solve the complication. Only then

do you move on to explain how this position has arisen (situation) and how it can be solved (key message). Your attitude clearly is empathic.

3 **Start with the situation for the jury:** 'Ladies and gentlemen, this was the situation. Supermarket X had a complication.' By sketching the situation first, you keep the emotional aspects of the situation under control. Then you can move on to explain the complication and the solution (key message). Your attitude is more factual, analytical and neutral.

Most presenters use this last approach. Personally, I like this approach least for business presentations. Why? Because, there is just too little emotion.

The introduction is also a good moment to explain your setting to the audience. Tell them what they can expect; how long the presentation will take; how you will involve them; when you will ask questions.

The importance of a good first impression

Do you remember the story of Jess's job interview? How she made a bad first impression on me and how I still held this against her more than a year later? First impressions are always vital – and that applies equally for your presentation. John Medina gives a neurological explanation for this phenomenon in his book *Brain Rules* (Medina, 2009).

New information arrives in the central part of the brain, the hippocampus. This plays an important role in organising the brain's various tasks. It is here that information is split up into smaller chunks and sent off to different parts of the cortex. Medina compares it to a blender with the lid off: the information is spun off to the outer parts of our brain, where it is processed in many different places. It is the cortex and the hippocampus that carry out the tasks of the working memory.

However, the long-term memory is also located in the cortex. New neuro-imaging techniques allow us to identify where information is stored and retrieved. And what transpires? It seems that the information relating to each of our memories is spread over many different parts of the cortex. Various 'spots' light up when this information is recalled. But it also seems that these are precisely the same 'spots' where the first memory in a series of memories was stored.

In other words, neuro-imaging has established that successive phases of the same memory are stored in the same physical location within the brain. The first memory – or first impression – therefore acts as a kind of foundation on which all subsequent layers of the same memory are built. This is a possible neurological explanation for why a first impression is so important: it colours all later memories that are added on top of it.

The middle: the body of your story

To write the body of your story, first you take the pyramid structure that you made to organise the logic of your presentation. Alongside this you place the different handles you have selected. You run through the pyramid in sequential order, adding the handles where they seem most necessary or appropriate.

You must work from top to bottom. Start with your key message. Ask the related question and give the different answers to this question. These are the 'chapters' of your presentation.

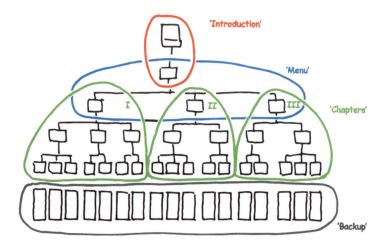

Use the pyramid structure to subdivide your presentation

Then you can move on to discuss these answers one by one. You carry on explaining each level in the same way, adding a handle every now and then, often as the introduction or conclusion of a section.

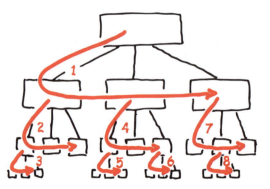

Start with key messages and general ideas before going into the details

It is crucial that you find a good way to pass from one answer to the next. In particular, it is useful, before passing to another box in your map, to summarise the content of the level above:

'… This was the first reason why the ROI of this project is guaranteed to be positive. As I said earlier, there were two other reasons for this, namely …….. and …….., so now let's look at the second reason …'

This is where a summary slide with the first level (or the first two levels) of your pyramid structure will prove its value. You can show this slide at each transition moment. It acts as a kind of table of contents for your entire presentation. It details your key message and the different 'chapters', each of which is an answer to the same question. In this way, you will help your audience to follow the logical line of your reasoning. At the same time, it also allows you to repeat your key message and its underlying arguments, a neat trick that helps to hammer home your message all the more firmly. Repetition is an important weapon when you want to lodge a piece of information in someone's memory. This has been a standard procedure in education for centuries.

When this is done, the body of your presentation is more or less complete. All you need to do now is add a powerful conclusion.

The importance of repetition

All memories are forgotten eventually. But fresh memories are especially vulnerable. The way our long-term memory stores information is different from the way a computer saves data or the way a person puts away a document in a filing cabinet. A 'fresh' memory is still very volatile and can be forgotten easily.

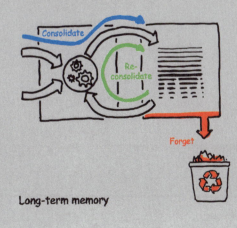

Regular repetition helps to stabilise a memory and imprint it more firmly into your mind (this is called consolidation). There are three different types of repetition: you can repeat the message, you can bring the message back into the working memory by recalling it and you can 'remember' the message in your sleep. The last two methods are known as 'reconsolidation'.

You can compare the technique of consolidating a memory with painting a wall. If you have ever used paint and brush in your own home, you will know that you don't apply paint in a single thick layer. First you apply a thin layer of undercoat and let it dry. Then you add a second layer and let that dry as well. Sometimes you add a third, fourth or even fifth layer, always allowing them sufficient time to dry. The longer you want your paint to last and the nicer you want it to look, the more layers you use.

We remember things in much the same way. You can't shovel information into your memory; you need to spoon it in, a little bit at a time. And you need to leave regular pauses in between, so that the information has time to settle. This is why you have to repeat your key message at periodic intervals. Your pyramid structure is the ideal tool for this purpose. Every time you move to a next section it gives you the perfect opportunity to remind people about the messages in the 'layer' above. Do this explicitly throughout the course of your presentation.

The end: a flexible conclusion

You don't need a long conclusion. Your listeners have followed your reasoning closely and they have heard your key message several times. If you have done this properly, they will be convinced already. Nevertheless, you need to round off your story in some way and double-check that you have achieved your goal. So link that conclusion to the goal you have set in Phase 1:

Know:

- **Repeat the key message (again).** Make a short statement that summarises your key message for a final time. If necessary, you can also recapitulate the next level, but go no further than that.

Do:

- **Call-to-action.** Ask your audience explicitly to take action: organise a discussion, take a decision, pass the information on to their team, etc.

- **Commitment.** Ask your audience explicitly if they agree. Saying 'yes' out loud will help to make sure that they actually do what you have asked. This is one of Robert Cialdini's six methods of influencing.

Feel:

- **Emotion.** Make an emotional appeal. Reactivate and name the emotions that you have linked to your message: 'We are in great danger ...', 'Urgent action is necessary ...', 'Let's celebrate our success ...', 'Rest reassured that ...'

- **Philosophical insight or a higher goal.** Since your key message should, by now, be clear, you can raise your audience to a higher level by offering them a philosophical insight. 'What does this really mean for the world?' or 'Yes, I am asking for extra budget, but our real purpose in the end is the well-being of our customers.'

A conclusion must always be short and must be capable of being used at different moments in your presentation. After all, you might have less time than you were promised. If this happens, it is important that you can still finish with a clinching finale.

Tips for the flexible use of your conclusion

1. See your conclusion as a *passe-partout* that can be inserted at any level in your pyramid.

2. Use your conclusion only after completing a full step in your pyramid. Avoid rounding off when you are only half way through a logical group.

3. Look in advance to see where you can use your conclusion. If you know that time is going to be tight, decide the best place to break off. If your pyramid is well designed, every level under that point can be dropped, and your reasoning will still hold. The audience will hardly notice that your presentation is shorter than you planned!

4. Hang on to your handles. Don't be tempted to cut out all your handles to shorten the presentation. If you do this, you might lose the audience's attention. This is far worse than not being able to pass on all the details.

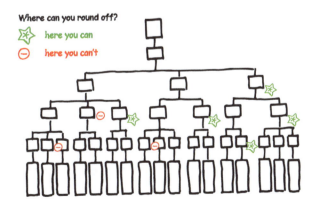

Where can you round off?
⭐ here you can
⊖ here you can't

HOW DO YOU DO ALL THIS IN PRACTICE?

That was the theory – but how do you write a storyline in practice? Everyone has their own preference. Here are a few options:

As A5 Cards   Outline in a text document   In your presentation software

How do you write out your speaker notes?

- **Word processors** are useful for putting together your story in the form of an outline. You indent the text each time you pass to a lower level of your pyramid structure. However, sheets of A4 are a bit cumbersome if you plan to use them as a guide during your talk.

- **Pen and paper** (traditionalists will be pleased to note) can also do the job. Often I use A5 or A6 or filing cards. You can note down a different part of your story on each card and they are handy to use on the day. Once they are in the right order, number them: you wouldn't be the first speaker to drop them just before your presentation!

- **Notes in the presentation software.** If you work directly in the presentation software, work as follows:

    - **Note down the titles of all your slides.** The titles are the key messages that you noted down in the different boxes of your pyramid. You can add these titles immediately to your slides in PowerPoint. The titles are the theme of your story.

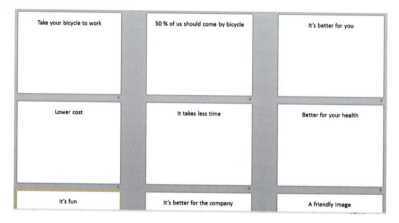

– **Write the storyline** in the boxes for speaker notes. You will design the slides later on. It is only when you know what to you want to say that you can design the slide itself. Never do this the other way around! Making speaker notes before making the slides helps you to resist the temptation to put too much text on your slides.

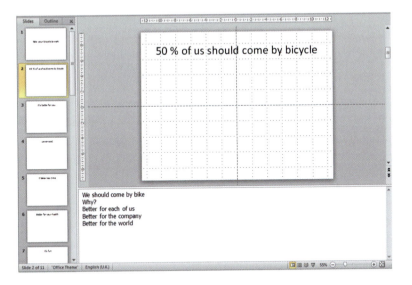

Don't forget: we are talking here about the narrative part of your presentation, the things you are actually going to say. This is *not* what will appear on your slides. You make them later on.

Whichever method you use, it is better not to write out full sentences. Short points or aide-memoires are all you need. During your presentation, you are supposed to be telling a story in your own words – not reading out a written text!

The exceptions to this rule are your first and last sentences. These should be written out in full. As should your key message. And you should know them by heart. During the crucial moments of your presentation, you don't want to waste time and nervous energy thinking about the words you need use.

CAPTURE AND HOLD THEIR ATTENTION

At the start of this chapter you read how attention works. Your storyline must ensure that you capture and keep your audience's attention. People remain attentive if they think that something is important or interesting. This is why meaning is always more important than detail. The human brain loves hierarchy. Before it is ready to deal with details, first it wants to see the broad outlines; only then will it decide whether or not there is sufficient interest to warrant its continued attention.

This underlines the importance of building your presentation structure top-down, working from the highest level of abstraction towards the lowest level of detail. This is the order in which you must present your information. Or, to quote Medina: 'Whether you are a waiter or a brain scientist, if you want to get the particulars correct, don't start with details. Start with the key ideas and, in a hierarchical fashion, form the details around these larger notions' (Medina, 2008).

Attention is fleeting. Even if the audience wants to remain attentive, sooner or later (usually sooner) their attention will begin to wander. When the interest is high, attention can be maintained for about 10 to 15 minutes. From then on, it's all downhill.

For this reason, it is useful to break up your presentation into blocks of about 10 minutes. After each block, you need to 'bribe' your audience into giving you back their attention. This is where your handles come in useful. An interesting example, a story, a surprise, a joke or an interactive exercise: they can all help to refocus lost attention. So, remember to do this every 10 minutes throughout your presentation.

Using questions is another easy way to maintain attention. Because you have used the Minto Pyramid Principle, all your material is already arranged in question-and-answer form. This gives your presentation a natural feel, almost like a conversation. Sometimes you can answer your own questions, sometimes let someone from the audience do it or let several of them make a guess, before you give the right answer.

DON'T FORGET THE SENSORY DETAILS

Earlier on I explained the concept of sensory integrations. It bears repeating: sensory stimuli help to encode information more deeply in our memory. This is something you can exploit to your benefit.

If you are giving a presentation about customer friendliness or a description of a new target group, don't limit yourself to vague and meaningless descriptions. Build in emotive elements. Your new customer is not a '55-plus mid-segment' but is a real person!

> 'He is a somewhat older man, who lives with his wife in a large house. The children (two sons) are both married and have well-paid jobs. He still feels virile, but knows that his best years are behind him. He wears an old tweed jacket. You know the type: lots of money, but doesn't like spending it. That is why he now has a £4.5 million sitting in the bank and he follows the stock market daily ...'

This is no longer an anonymous customer, but a real-life, flesh-and-blood person. If you use this type of information, your listeners will understand better what you really mean. It is almost as if they know the person, and this will help them to understand what he wants, needs and feels.

Presenting like Hercule Poirot should be the exception

Do not attempt to present like me.

You will fail, unless you possess the exquisite quality of creating a true mystery.

Mysteries are super-charged surprises. Only if you can succeed in turning your presentation into a mystery, it may be possible to keep your key message, your final conclusion, right to the very end. Much like Hercule Poirot.

In this case, the mystery you create must have an exceptional emotional force. And your audience must be sitting on the edge of their seats, dying to know the answer. It must occupy their thoughts completely.

We experience something as a mystery when there is a 'gap' in our knowledge. There is something we don't know and we have a compulsion to find out what it is. It is interesting to note that the smaller the 'gap', the more anxious we are to have it filled! Or, to put it differently: the more your audience knows about a subject, the more they are interested to know about those last few remaining bits they didn't know.

Imagine that you know two or three of last weekend's football results. You will find it amusing, probably, to display your 'knowledge' at coffee on Monday morning. Especially if you are not known as a football fan. But, if you are a real football fanatic and you know all the weekend's results except one, you will be frantic to know what it is.

This means that mysteries only work in groups with a very high level of prior knowledge and an exceptionally high degree of interest in the subject. In this case, you can screw up the tension by keeping part of the answer to the very end. In all other cases, it is wiser to do the exact opposite.

IN SHORT

Your story is ready! You have described it all concisely in bullet points. You have written out the most important sentences in full. You have used your 'lead' as an introduction. For the middle section, you have used your pyramid structure, running top-down through the levels. You have added handles at regular intervals. And you have written a conclusion that can be inserted at different points in the pyramid, depending on the time you have available.

PHASE 4
THE MEDIA
How do you reinforce the story?

SLIDES – DOCUMENTS – GET READY!

How can we improve internal communication? In the spring of 2011, a large financial organisation was asking just that question. Its system of communication was then as follows: each month the different departments put together documents with all relevant information for distribution to more than 25,000 staff. This was done centrally in the head office. All the information was placed on slides and brought together in a single large presentation that subsequently was distributed to hundreds of different locations.

It was intended that all managers at all locations should show the slides – some 250 in all – to their staff, so that the information would filter down gradually through the hierarchy. This kind of information 'waterfall' is not uncommon in the business world.

The slides were made 'both to read and to present'. But staff with busy agendas don't really have time to read 250 slides. And a monthly team meeting with 250 slides would take two days rather than two hours. So, most managers made a selection from the slides. As a result, everyone was seeing incomplete information and there was little common vision.

Amongst other measures, they decided to entrust the making of slides to just half a dozen employees. The number of slides was reduced to about 40! The information per slide was also cut by half. The new style slides were more visually attractive and, above all, much clearer. All the staff thought it was a huge improvement: the information was more understandable, the meetings were more interesting, and there was also time for discussion. None of the regional managers saw any need to 'amend' the new slides. But were people now receiving less information? Not at all. Because the 40 slides were accompanied by a more detailed document of 20 to 25 pages that summarised what everybody needed to know. It was a huge improvement on 250 slides!

The time saving was also huge. Forty hours was enough to make the new-style slides and an appendix. Previously, the task had taken more than three times as long!

'Language is the glove that is pulled tightly over the skin of content.' Godfried Bomans

In this fourth phase you have arrived in the finishing straight. Most of the work is behind you. You know what you want to achieve, what logical information you will convey and which sensory elements you need. In fact, you are ready to get up and speak to your audience. Well, almost. In most business presentations you also need a number of visual tools. This can be a powerpoint or some other visual aid. But, whichever tool you use, remember that its role is, essentially, supportive.

For large audiences it is practical to use a powerpoint. For smaller groups of three to four people, a flip chart can be enough. You can also make use of videos, sound recordings, a whiteboard, a smart board or, even, (my favourite) an old-fashioned blackboard and chalk. Similarly, you can work with a syllabus, handouts or other more sophisticated tools.

To decide which medium is best, consider the following criteria:

- **The effectiveness of the medium.** What is most suitable for your needs?
- **Company culture.** If you are giving a presentation in a company where powerpoints are the norm, it is best if you do the same.
- **Cost.** Don't invest in (expensive) 3D video if you are going to use it only once.
- **Available time.** You have only five minutes. How many slides can you show?

- **Knowledge of the medium.** Don't use a smart board if you're not sure how it works.

- **The experience you wish to give.** Do you want to surprise? Then use a surprising medium; for example, the more innovative Prezi rather than the more standard PowerPoint. But remember that not everyone is as proficient as you with the most advanced technical options. Prezi's 'infinite canvas' might be beyond their ability.

TO POWERPOINT OR NOT TO POWERPOINT?

I already mentioned this in Part I. It makes little difference which software program you use for the majority of business presentations. If you respect the rules of good slide design, each of the software programs has its merits. The difference is, primarily, in the interface. Some are more user-friendly than others. The most important thing is that you are familiar with it and can use it to maximum effect with a minimum of time.

There has been much criticism of the use of PowerPoint, but this is not always justified. As Don Norman put it in his essay 'In Defense of PowerPoint': 'There were boring presentations long before PowerPoint came along,' (Norman, 2004). The problem is not the technology, but the speaker. Speakers who read off text from their slides simply are not doing their job properly. They will lose their audience during the first few minutes.

Conclusion: take account of the above criteria and choose the medium that you are most comfortable with.

Tips for the better use of presentation software

1   Invest time in getting to know the software thoroughly. Soon you will win back the time, if you use the software regularly.

2   Learn the program's shortcuts. Also this will save you time.

3   Make use of a professional designer for your really important presentations. You will achieve better results more quickly than if you do it yourself.

More information? My website **www.edgruwez.com** will help you on your way.

STEP 10
Create your slides
Keep it minimal

'Make sure your slides don't compete with your words.'

Mackiewicz

The case of the financial organisation at the beginning of this phase is just one of many examples of how good slides improve communication and are quicker to make.

Even so, the making of good slides always demands time and attention. The most important question (again) is what you want to achieve with your slides. I distinguish between four different types, each of which takes a different amount of time and effort to prepare:

- Keynote slides – for large, important presentations.
- Meeting slides – for presentations for smaller groups.
- Working slides – as a collaborative tool to develop insights.
- Information slides – for back-up information.

Each type has different requirements. Let's have a look.

- **Keynote slides.** These slides must be as visually strong as possible. You want a perfect graphic design, but without tricks and frills. Avoid text, so that attention is focused on the words of the speaker. Keynote slides often don't even need titles. The message is given verbally by the speaker. Pay proper attention to the animations, so that the visual elements appear at exactly the right moment. The graphic finishing must be impeccable. Never give keynote slides to the audience after the presentation.

- **Meeting slides.** These slides allow more text and detail. Even so, limit the text to what is essential and never use full sentences; the slides are there only to underline what you say. Meeting slides nearly always have a title. The titles give structure to your presentation and summarise the content on the slide. Handouts usually are welcome in business meetings.

- **Working slides.** Use these slides during creative collaborative processes. The focus is not on the 'speaker' but on the output resulting from the interaction. For this reason, you can put more information on the slides; they are work documents rather than presentation slides. Never use these slides in real presentations. They can serve as a basis, but will need thorough reworking.

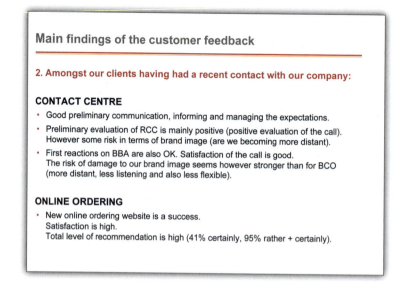

Main findings of the customer feedback

2. Amongst our clients having had a recent contact with our company:

CONTACT CENTRE
- Good preliminary communication, informing and managing the expectations.
- Preliminary evaluation of RCC is mainly positive (positive evaluation of the call). However some risk in terms of brand image (are we becoming more distant).
- First reactions on BBA are also OK. Satisfaction of the call is good. The risk of damage to our brand image seems however stronger than for BCO (more distant, less listening and also less flexible).

ONLINE ORDERING
- New online ordering website is a success. Satisfaction is high. Total level of recommendation is high (41% certainly, 95% rather + certainly).

- **Information slides.** These slides are used to answer technical questions. As a result, the layout is less important. Efficiency is what counts. You can fill the slides with data, tables and graphics with minimal layout. Use information slides if you want to show that your presentation is based on solid facts and figures. Don't leave this data too long on screen during the actual presentation. You don't want your audience to try and read all the details!

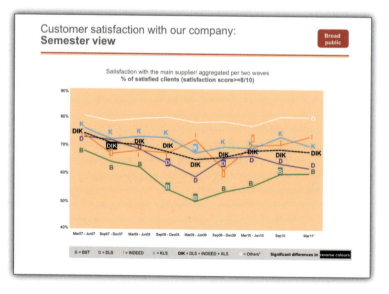

HOW DO YOU START MAKING SLIDES?

When you are designing your own slides, start by remembering that layout is subordinate to the clarity and appeal of your ideas. Your story must be right; that is more important than your slides. If time is tight, design 'minimalist' slides. Or dispense with slides altogether. Why do people always want to use digital tools for their presentations, when a whiteboard or a flip chart are much easier? But don't forget to make a predesign, even for flip-chart drawings. Check that you are actually capable of drawing the things you want to draw within a reasonable amount of time – by using a flip chart, you give a more natural impression.

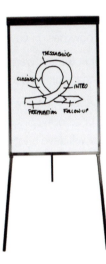

Some people find flip charts impractical, because you don't have any handouts for after the presentation. With a little creativity, this objection can be overcome easily. Use your smartphone's camera to take photos of your sketches on the flip chart or whiteboard. Add them to a Word document with a little extra explanation and, within half an hour, your handout will be ready and you can mail it to your participants.

When you finally start work on your slides, I would recommend you use one of the following two procedures: PowerPoint–Paper–Powerpoint (digital–analogue–digital) or Paper–PowerPoint (analogue–digital). The essential point about both methods is that first you design your slides on paper and not directly in the software. Think of yourself as an architect: he also puts his ideas down in a sketch before he elaborates them in CAD.

Digital – analogue – digital

Digital

If you have written your storyline in the speaker notes of your presentation program, you have done this first step already. If not, copy your storyline to the speaker notes and add the title into the slides.

Analogue

1 **Print off a blank storyboard** by printing your slides and speaker notes. Two or three per page. This gives you a kind of storyboard, like film directors use. The sheets with blank slides are the worksheets on which you can now design your individual slide content.

2 **Draw your slides.** Do it on paper, not in the software program. Work with a pencil and an eraser, so that you can change things that don't work easily.

3 **Check.** Once everything is down on paper, you have a good working document that you can use to rehearse or to check with your boss or a colleague. By doing that now – instead of when the slides have been made – you will save a lot of time.

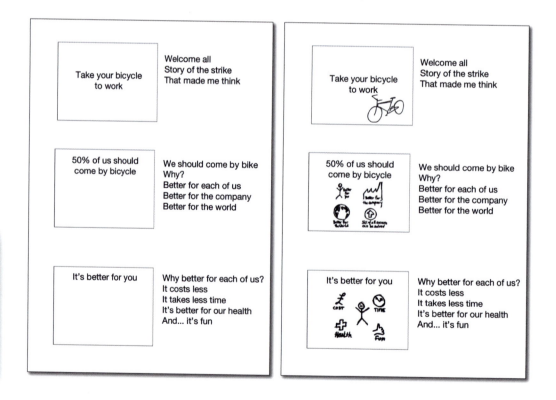

Digital

1 Now you can start making your slides in the presentation software. Remember to keep the cognitive load as low as possible; scrap anything that is not relevant.

2 View your slides critically. When you have finished designing your slides in PowerPoint or another software program, first look through the slideshow yourself. Be critical:

– Is each slide really necessary? Do you have doubts? Hide the slide; you can still call it up during the presentation if you need to.

– Is everything on the slide really necessary? Have you used too much text? Are there images, words and graphics that are really just ballast? If so, delete them.

– Check the slides with your boss or colleagues.

3 Work on the build-up and the animation. It is a good idea to leave the animation right to the very end. This will save you lots of time if changes are necessary. Check carefully through your speaker notes. What are you going to say? Make sure that the right visual elements appear at the right moment, so that the attention of your audience is focused on what you say.

Analogue – digital

The second approach is not so very different from the first. You just miss out the first PowerPoint step and note down your titles and speaker notes directly on paper. Use some sheets of A5 paper (just cut some A4 sheets in two). Write the title on the top of each sheet and then design your slide underneath it. This will give you one sheet of paper for each slide. Number the pages.

You can practise your presentation with this paper version. Once you are satisfied that everything is as it should be, you can transfer the paper version into your presentation program. This is the quickest method of working, and the one I use most often.

And, if you jot down the speaker notes on the back of your paper 'slides', immediately you have a handy bundle that you can use during the presentation.

PAPER DESIGN

FINAL SLIDE

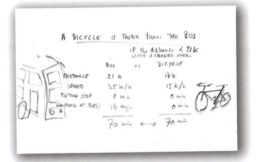

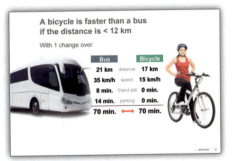

DIGITAL – ANALOGUE – DIGITAL	ANALOGUE – DIGITAL
Digital	**Analogue**
• Put titles at the top of the slides	• Take sheets of A5 paper
• Copy key messages into the speaker notes boxes	• Write the title at the top of each sheet
Analogue	• Write what you will say on the back of each sheet
• Print blank slides with speaker notes	• Design the slides with pencil and eraser
• Design slides with pencil and eraser	• Test the presentation on paper
• Test the presentation on paper	**Digital**
Digital	• Design the slides in the software
• Design the slides in the software	• Check the presentation
• Check the presentation	• Add the animation
• Add the animation	

The quick and easy way from pyramid structure to slides

The pyramid structure gives you a good indication of what can appear on each slide. In fact, you can make one slide for each group in the structure. The summary statement is the title and the different elements in the group appear on the slide, preferably in a visual way or with bullets.

STEP 10
SLIDES

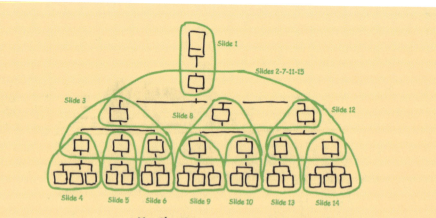

Use the structure map to design slides quickly

If you closely follow the pyramid, this will immediately make the structure of your talk clear to the audience. And if your map is well-designed, it will also give you a good set of slides without too much effort. Even so, following this logic too strictly might result in a dull presentation. You can alternate by putting three levels instead of 2 on one slide and add extra slides to visually support anecdotes and other handles.

Five reasons to design slides on paper

1 **It empties your mind.** Drawing is a relaxing activity that stimulates your creativity. And creativity is what you need to design top slides that support your message.

2 **You free up cognitive energy.** Working with a software program uses up lots of cognitive capacity. So work on paper instead and focus on sketching your slides. Don't get bogged down in the technicality of your software.

3 **Drawing saves time.** You can draw much more quickly on paper than in a computer program.

4 **You are more critical about the result.** PowerPoint always looks good in your own eyes. You are not going to delete a slide on which you have just spent almost one hour to make, are you?

5 **You design simple slides.** If you work on paper, you will soon notice that you put less on each slide. It's difficult to explain why, but it's true!

BE CAREFUL WITH TEMPLATES

Many companies work with mandatory templates. There is a house style that everybody must use. Usually this is more of a curse than a blessing. The templates are attractive – that is not the problem – but they are often unsuitable for presentations. They are designed by communication managers, who primarily are concerned with emphasising the company logo and making visually "pretty" slides. To make matters worse, frequently they contain unnecessary information.

Templates are designed seldom with presentations in mind. In particular, the designers overlook the need to keep cognitive load to a minimum. Just check out a few examples online: many contain 'heavy' cognitive elements that add little to your presentation (a logo on each side, many coloured elements, the company's web address, a disclaimer, advertising banners, etc.). This takes up lots of valuable space, both on your slides and in the brain of the listener.

And, if you follow the dictates of the template meekly, you end up with a kind of boring uniformity. All the presentations look like visual clones that have everyone nodding off in boredom. Be bold and use your creativity to turn the limitations of the template to your advantage. Minor alterations usually are allowed, as long as you respect the house style. But don't take things too far. I am not preaching template revolution! I understand fully the concerns of most communication managers. Giving everyone the freedom to 'do their own thing' leads to pretty dodgy presentations. So, yes, templates are here to stay and quite right too! But allow them to be made by graphic designers who know a thing or two about making presentations.

Tips for template designers

1 **Don't overdo it with the logo.** Is the logo really necessary? On every slide? Clearly this is not the case for internal presentations. People know what company they are working for. Even for external presentations, it must be possible to limit the number and size within reasonable bounds.

2 **Choose your colours.** Allow the presenter to choose from different colour palettes. This will avoid the use of inappropriate colour combinations and will prevent all presentations from looking the same.

3 **Limit cognitive load.** Design the template so that people's working memories need to make minimal mental effort. This means limiting the number of visual elements. Make them attractive, but also make sure that they don't attract the viewers' attention away from other more important elements.

4 **Build up your own image bank.** Help the presenter to find good and suitable images. If you have your own image bank, you will save him time and the visuals will have the 'look and feel' that you want. Provide images with maximum resolution, so that the user can enlarge and cut them to suit his needs.

BAD

BETTER

TITLE SLIDES

Design slides that make the structure of your talk and the transition from subject to the next crystal clear. These are your 'title slides' or 'menu slides'. They offer you a unique chance to repeat your key message. Leave them on the screen whilst you tell an anecdote or another bridge to the next subject.

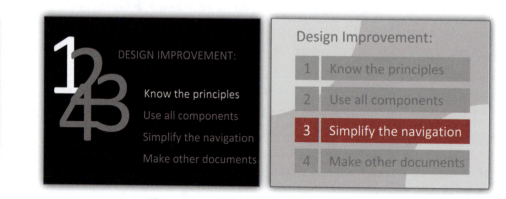

SLIDE GRAVEYARD

Often you will find that a slide is not necessary, but it pains you to have to delete it altogether. Make a slide graveyard at the end of your presentation, where you can temporarily 'bury' all your beautiful outtakes. You can download this fun title slide for a slide graveyard from my website.

FIND THE RIGHT LEVEL FOR YOUR GRAPHIC DESIGN

A graphic design can tell more than you might think. A poor graphic design will make the audience feel uncomfortable. Does the speaker think that the subject isn't important enough to make something better? Or that his audience has time to waste on this kind of sub-standard trash? But make sure you don't go too far in the opposite direction. If your graphic design is too state-of-the-art, you open yourself to other kinds of criticism: 'That must have cost a bomb!' or 'Well, that was triumph of form over substance!'. This last situation sometimes arises when the presenter has used a graphic designer who knows everything about graphics but nothing about presentations!

The principles of multimedia design

Richard Mayer carried out extensive scientific research into the use of multimedia (slides in particular) in a learning process. In his book *Multimedia Learning* he summarised his conclusions in 12 multimedia design principles (Mayer, 2009). In part, these principles are explained by the theory of the working memory and all have been proved to have a solid scientific foundation. The first 10 of these principles are useful for the design of presentation slides. (The last two are relevant only for e-learning, and therefore do not concern us.)

PRINCIPLE	MEANING
Coherence	People learn and understand better when all unnecessary text, images and sound are removed.
Signalling	People learn and understand better when signals are given that direct their attention and clarify the organisation of the content.
Redundancy	People learn better with graphic elements and spoken text than with graphic elements, spoken text and text on screen.
Spatial contingency	People learn and understand better when related text and images are close together on the screen rather than far apart.
Temporal contingency	People learn and understand better when related text and images appear on the screen at the same time rather than one after the other.
Segmenting	People learn and understand better when the content is presented one item at a time, at the user's own pace, rather than as a continuous whole.
Pre-training	People learn and understand better when they know the names and principles of the most important concepts in advance.
Modality	People learn better with images accompanied by a narrated story than with images accompanied by a story in text form.
Multimedia	People learn better with words and images than with words alone.
Personalisation	People learn and understand better when words are used in a conversational style rather than a formal style.

Source: Adapted from tables 14.1, 14.2 and 14.3 (pages 267–268) in Richard E Mayer, Multimedia Learning, *2nd Edition, © Richard E Mayer 2001, 2009, published by Cambridge University Press, adapted with permission.*

THE BASIC PRINCIPLES OF GRAPHIC DESIGN

You don't need to be an expert graphic designer to make a good business presentation. For an important keynote presentation, it is, perhaps, advisable to hire the services of a professional for the design of your slides, and preferably one that specialises in presentations.

But, for standard business presentations, you can make slides of the required standard simply by applying a number of basic graphic design principles. The most important of these are:

- use of the available space;
- use of text in slides;
- use of colour;
- use of images: forms, diagrams, photos and video;
- visualising data: graphics and tables;
- animations and interactions.

Use of the available space

So, here you are, with your blank sheet of paper. What are you going to put on it? And where are you going to put it? The most obvious first step is to put the title at the top. Underneath you should add in the elements that relate to that group title, in the order in which you intend to talk about them. But where will they appear on the screen during the presentation? That can be from top to bottom, but it doesn't have to be that way. The most important thing is that the available space on the screen is used to best advantage, in a manner that attracts the 'eye' of your listeners towards the things that are most important. Think about it. What will your listener look at first? And what next? Images attract attention, as do bright colours, large text and anything that is unexpected.

But don't forget the importance of white space. Most speakers seem to be afraid of large areas of white space on their slides, just like they hate long silences. Yet both of these things have a positive effect on your presentation. They provide a moment's rest and allow your audience to concentrate on the things that really matter. So resist the temptation to fill every square centimetre of space on every slide. With full slides the participants waste a lot of their cognitive capacity working out where the different elements are located. This leaves only a small bit of that capacity for the more important task of listening. If you have a really full slide, turn it into several slides, each with less information.

How do you divide up the available space in a harmonious way?

1   Using two horizontal and two vertical lines, divide your slide into nine rectangles. Align texts and
other elements on the lines, intersections or planes of this grid.

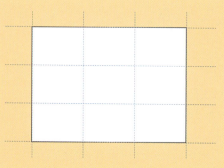

2   Use the golden ratio to divide your slide, a line or a plane into unequal parts. The ratio between the
larger and the smaller part is the same as the ratio between the larger part and the whole.

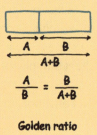

Golden ratio

Use of text in slides

People understand things better when it is explained to them verbally with the use of
accompanying images. Even so, often you need to use text on a slide. You must regard your
slide as a kind of road sign. It is nothing more than an indicator, which you look at to make sure
that you can carry out the correct traffic manoeuvre. If you need too much time to read the road
sign, you will cause an accident. So, write text on your slide the same way you would write text
on a road sign. Make sure it is legible.

Can you read your slides at 60 km/h?

Tips for better text on slides

1 **Don't use full sentences on slides.** Don't write everything you will say verbally. Just use key words that serve as a visual and support your message. Check each slide to see how you can make the text more compact. Scrap as much as you can.

2 **Remember to consider the spacing of the text.** Leave sufficient white space between the different text elements.

3 **Don't put frames around your text.** This looks nice, but the frame considerably increases the cognitive load. Use frames only on very simple slides or to emphasise your key message.

4 **Make sure there is enough contrast between your text and the background.** This is an important factor in legibility.

5 **Use text as a visual element.** Play with colour and size. It is a simple but effective way to make a visually powerful slide.

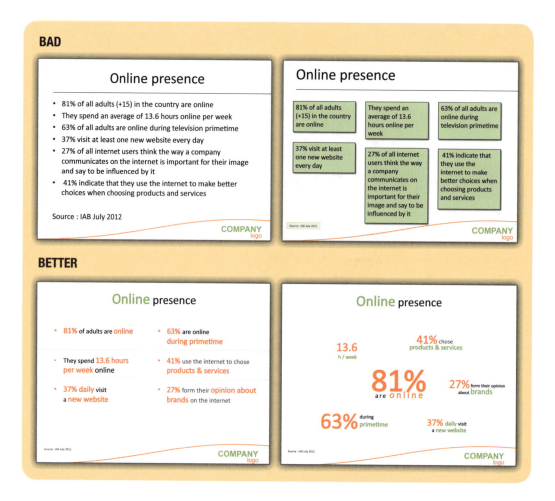

Spatial proximity

Objects that belong together logically should also be positioned close together. A group of American researchers discovered that students found it more difficult to understand mathematical formulae when the text and the graphic representation of the formulae were separated from each other.

This confirms Mayer's 'spatial contingency' principle. Designers prefer to refer to this as 'spatial proximity' but, in essence, both terms mean the same thing: images and words that belong together should be positioned as close as possible to each other. In this way, the relationship between the two becomes more obvious.

About fonts and sizes

Nowadays, all software packages offer a wide range of fonts. It is tempting to play with some of these, but don't – unless you really know what you are doing.

1 **Choose legible fonts.** Serif letter types like Times or Garamond are best for printed texts. Sans serif letter types like Arial or Verdana are better for use on screens.

2 **Choose standard fonts for your program.** Or embed it in your presentation. If you don't, then the font might be replaced with another one, messing up the layout.

3 **Make your font large enough.** In the vast majority of presentations the letter size is too small. Adjust the size according to your audience. For a large group you need a large letter size. How large? Go to the back of the room and look for yourself. Can you read the text easily? The general rule is: the bigger the room, the bigger your text must be.

STEP 10
SLIDES

Text or no text on slides?

In Part I – the chapter about the working memory – you read that the brain can process auditory and visual information separately from each other.

You also know that reading demands greater cognitive effort. With reading, you must transfer visually recognised information to your auditory memory. Why? Because language (in evolutionary terms) is an auditory medium, so that our language centre is located in the auditory working memory. This is also why, as a child, you first learnt to read out loud before you learnt to read silently. Written text monopolises both the visual and the auditory memory channels. This means that it is impossible for your audience to read text on a screen and listen to you at the same time.

With single words this is not such a problem. Thanks to our automatic recognition processes, a single word doesn't require the auditory memory. As a result, single words are an effective way to strengthen your key message, particularly if you use the same words in your talk.

If, for whatever reason, you do need to write a full sentence on a slide – for example, a quotation or your company's mission statement – read it out loud or give your audience time to read it themselves, before you carry on further with what you were saying.

Use of colour

Choosing the right colour plays a major role in making your slides visually attractive; but can also increase the cognitive load unnecessarily. Play with colours, by all means, but do it carefully. If you want to know more about the best way to use and combine colours, there is plenty of information on the internet and dozens of books on graphic design.

Before preparing your slides, it is a good idea first to make a separate slide with your colour palette. How do you choose the colours you need? Well, you can start with the logo of the company where you are giving your presentation or, if you have used a photo with your key message, use some of the colours from that photo.

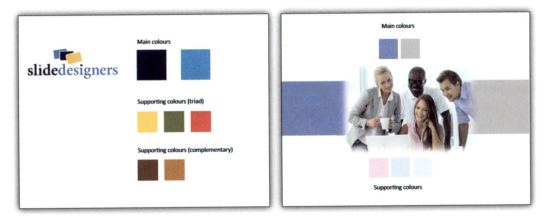

Do you always need colour? Not really. Consider doing a presentation in just grey tints. It gives a professional impression and, by adding coloured elements here and there, you can emphasise specific things for your audience.

BAD

BETTER

BAD

BETTER

Tips to improve your choice of colour

1 **Limit the number of colours** from three to a maximum of five. More than five makes your slide too complex and too visually oppressive.

2 **Use the same colours** throughout the presentation. Select a harmonious colour palette and stick to it.

3 **Choose colours that harmonise well.** Nothing creates a more 'messy' impression than colours that are chosen without thought. Use the colour wheel that you can find in most layout programs:

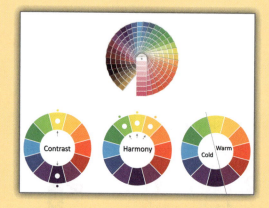

- Colours that are opposite each other in the wheel have the highest contrast.
- Colours that are at an equal distance from each other often go well together.
- Cold and warm colours each fill half the wheel. Warm colours bring objects to the foreground, so use these for objects you want to accentuate. Cold colours are more suited for backgrounds or for things you don't need to emphasise.

Some programs or websites have a tool that will help you to put together a harmonious palette.

This is more
difficult to read
on the screen

While this
is much
easier to read

4 **Avoid 'almost-colours'.** Do you want to use the colours of a logo or a photograph in your presentation? If so, don't try to choose this colour from a colour wheel, because then, almost certainly, you will end up with an 'almost-colour'. Instead, use a 'colour picker' that allows you to copy different tints perfectly.

5 **Take account of the projection quality.** Most projectors show less contrast than the screen of a computer. Also, colours can differ from one piece of equipment to another. Soft pastel shades that looked great in your design sometimes become almost invisible on screen. If possible, test your presentation in situ on the projector you are going to use. If necessary, you can then recolour certain elements.

6 **Don't forget the colour-blind!** 15 to 18 per cent of all men are colour-blind. (The figure is less than 1 per cent for women.) Colour-blind people find it hard to distinguish the contrast between certain colours. You can check that your slides will be seen easily by everybody by looking at them first in black and white. Slides in exclusively grey tints are legible for everyone.

Look on **www.edgruwez.com** for more details.

The effect of colour on communication

Numerous researchers, such as Tim Smits (Smits, 2013) and Meyers and Peracchio (Meyers, 1995), have studied the use of colour in advertising. They looked at the way people reacted to four-colour adverts, black and white adverts or adverts with a spot colour. All the research produced the same results:

- If interest for the advertised product is low, the four-colour version attracts more attention.

- If interest for the product is high, colours have a negative effect. They increase the cognitive load and deflect attention from the key message, especially if they are used for subsidiary elements.

- If just a spot colour is added to an otherwise black and white advertisement, the colour does not have a distracting effect.

You can apply this knowledge when designing your slides. Give colour to the things you want to emphasise, but keep the surrounding tints sober (or even grey). If you want to attract attention to a particularly important slide, you can really pull out all the colour stops. But don't overdo it. If your presentation as a whole looks like Times Square on New Year's Eve, your audience won't know where to look first.

Tip: sprinkle breadcrumbs

With his Signalling Principle (one of Ten Principles for Multimedia Learning, based on research at the University of California), Richard Mayer advised making the structure of your story visible and showing, at any given moment, where you are in that structure. 'Breadcrumbs' is a good way to do this. They form a trail that your listener can follow. In websites it is common for this 'trail' to be placed at the top of each new page. In this way, the surfer knows where he is within the site.

You can do the same in a powerpoint, which is extremely useful in complex presentations. But don't make your breadcrumbs over-complicated. Often a reference to the first level in your pyramid structure is sufficient.

Although visuals are preferable, you can also use text as breadcrumbs. This is the simplest way and your audience knows the concept from websites.

Title of the presentation > name of the chapter > element within the chapter.

Use of images: forms, diagrams, photos and video

We looked at the use of images in Phase 3, with an emphasis on one or more visuals to support your key message. When we make slides, we are also creating images for the more detailed messages in our presentation. Of course, the principles remain the same.

Here are a few additional tips:

1 **Make sure there is a 'unity' throughout the presentation.** Your images and graphics must all have the same style. This creates 'rest' for your working memory and gives a good, professional impression.

2 **Avoid clichés and images that have been widely used already.** Many stock photos have been used a thousand times already. Be critical in your selection.

3 **Don't use a different photo for each slide.** This is confusing and cognitively 'heavy'. Choose fewer images that you can repeat in different slides.

4 **Vary your images according to subject** or the chapter you are in. If each chapter is characterised by a different image, this is an extra support for the memory of your listeners.

5 **Be careful with 3D and other special effects.** Presentation programs offer plenty of 3D options, shadows and other effects to make visuals and text graphically appealing. But, unless you do it well, it becomes confusing for your audience, so that cognitive load increases.

Some things to avoid are:

Too small

Badly positioned

Black outline

Bad resolution

Watermark

Stretched

Clipart and clichés

Text with a bad contrast

Distracting picture

A better example is:

Tips for good photos

Photos can be amended to suit the requirements of your presentation.

1 **Cut.** All presentation software has a tool that allows you to cut photos to size.

2 **Enlarge.** Large images make an impact, small ones don't. So don't be afraid to make your photos full-screen size.

3 **Colour.** Give unity to your photos by recolouring them. Most of the photos you want to use will have a different colour balance. You need to give them a more homogenous look.

4 **Black-and-white.** If you are not very good at balancing colours, opt for black-and-white. The images will attract less attention and will have a lower cognitive load.

5 **Text and image.** You can include text in your photos, certainly if they are page-size. But watch out for the following details:
    – Make sure there is sufficient contrast between text and image. This is easiest if the photo has an area that is either very dark or very light. Use a strongly contrasting text colour.
    – You can get the required contrast by placing a semi-transparent rectangle on top of the area on your photo where you want to add the text.

The following example shows how one photo can be adapted using the crop, remove background and enlarge tools in your presentation software.

Visualising data: graphics and tables

Business presentations make frequent use of numbers. Remember that it is your story that really counts, not showing all the numbers. Even so, often you will need to have numbers somewhere in your presentation.

It is not my intention to look at this in detail; there are specialist books, many of which are listed on my website. But you can go a long way with the following basic – and logical – tips, which take account of the theory of the working memory and minimal cognitive load.

Tips for tables

1 **Avoid over-large tables.** Limit the number of columns and rows. Use just enough information to make your point. No more, no less.

2 **Use as few horizontal and vertical lines as possible.** More lines mean more cognitive load. The same is true of heavily coloured zones.

3 **Use white space to separate columns and rows.** Use a slightly different background colour or replace the lines between rows with a light grey strip that doesn't attract attention.

4 **Guide the attention of your audience** to the numbers on which your conclusions are based.

This table is hard to read

	Total Client (JE)	% Client (JE)	ARPU (€)	Total revenus (€)	Segment contri-bution	Total Paid Fees (€)	Revenus Courtage (€)	Revenus Epargne (€)	Revenus Compte à Vue (€)
Active Traders	5.910	4%	2.575	16.992.646	40%	32%	3%	3	1%
Active Investors	16.040	11%	675	10.159.160	24%	11%	4%	7	2%
Small Investors	15.458	12%	146	2.401.624	6%	1,5%	2%	1	1%
Savers	11.485	8%	851	9.778.652	23%	0,3%	1%	19	2%
Small Savers	41.321	30%	65	9.699.382	6%	0%	1%	4	2%
Daily Bankers & Other products	49.015	39%	20	965.015	2%	0%	1%	0	1,6%
Total	139.229	100%	309	42.996.479	100%	19.597.364	4.743.182	14.792.999	3.862.934
						46%	11%	34%	9%

This table is much easier to read

	Total Client (K - J€)	% Client (J€)	ARPU (€)	Total revenus (M €)	Segment contri-bution	Total Paid Fees (% - M€)	Revenus Opte Courtage (% - M€)	Revenus Epargne (% - M€)	Revenus Compte à Vue (% - M€)
Active Traders	5.9	4%	2.575	17,0	40%	32%	3%	3	1%
Active Investors	15.0	11%	675	10.1	24%	11%	4%	7	2%
Small Investors	15.5	12%	146	2.4	6%	1,5%	2%	1	1%
Savers	11.5	8%	851	9.8	23%	0,3%	1%	19	2%
Small Savers	41.3	30%	65	9.7	6%	0%	1%	4	2%
Daily & Other	49.0	39%	20	1,0	2%	0%	1%	0	1,5%
Total	139.2	100%	309	43,0	100%	19.6	4.7	14.8	3.9

STEP 10
SLIDES

Tips for graphics

1 Choose the right type of graphic.
The type of graphic you use must reflect your reasoning or the conclusion you want to draw. There are different graphics for every different application.

Line:
for variables that change over time

Area:
for variables that change over time and that you can add over different periods

2 Put your conclusions next to the graphics. As close as possible, where they are visible. Better still, use no text. Let the graphics speak for themselves.

Column:
for all variables

3 Remove all lines that are not absolutely necessary. Every line means more cognitive load. Horizontal and vertical axes and grids usually are not necessary.

Bar:
for all variables
when you need more place for the names

Pie:
for parts of a whole

4 Avoid 3D and special effects. Most software offers these options, but they make the visual side of your presentation hopelessly complex.

Spider / Radar:
for 3-9 dimensions of one or more entities possibly compared to a norm

X-Y / Scatter:
to visualise a correlation

5 Be sparing with the use of colour.
Use the most eye-catching colours for the parts of the graphic you are talking about.

Bubble:
for 3 dimensions of data for multiple entities

6 Make different versions. When the same graphic contains different conclusions, use different colours or make the distinction clear in another way.

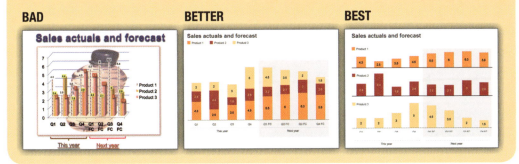

BAD   **BETTER**   **BEST**

STEP 10
SLIDES

Animations and interactions

Animations in a powerpoint are both a curse and a blessing. They are a blessing because of Mayer's 'Contiguity Principle'. In other words, you allow objects or text to become visible only at the moment you are talking about them. Animation or build-up makes this possible.

But animations can also be a curse, if they are ill-designed. The timing must be perfect and must be synchronised with your spoken text. Rotating, flashing or flying animations rarely offer added value. So, avoid the temptation to use these powerpoint effects. Remember the golden rule: keep it simple!

In general, you can use animations:

1 **To synchronise.** Use animation when you want an object to appear at the moment you are talking about a particular subject.

2 **To signal.** Movement attracts attention. This means you can use animations to focus attention on the element you are talking about.

3 **To simplify.** Animation not only allows you to make things appear and disappear, but also to move them around. Some processes become clearer with well-designed animation.

IN SHORT

At last! Now you have designed your slides. First on paper and then in your presentation program. Your design has taken account of a number of key principles about the use and positioning of text, the use of animations, etc. You have given the graphic aspects of your slides sufficient attention, but no more than that. If you are pressed for time, you can always resort to 'minimalist' slides. After all, it is the content that counts!

In all cases, keep the design of your slides as simple as possible; this will save you time and make things easier to understand for your audience.

STEP 11

Add your documents

Repeat your key message

In the example about the financial organisation at the beginning of Phase 4, we managed to cut the number of slides and the information they contained only by providing a supplementary document. This was a text document, in which the slides were used as illustrations. This reassured both the senders and the receivers that the information was complete, even with the drastic reduction in slides. After we had tested several alternatives, this seemed to be the most effective way to communicate the message concisely but completely. And also the most efficient, since the document was quick and easy to make, thanks to the slides.

You have a story to tell and your slides act as pictures in a book, to clarify and illustrate that story. But, often it can be useful to provide additional documentation, so that both you and your audience have a source of information. The extra documents you need will depend largely on what you want to achieve.

With most presentations there are three types of document that can give an added value:

- **Speaker notes**, as a memory aid for yourself or for others who will give the same presentation.
- **Handouts**, so that your audience can re-read what you said during the presentation.
- **Work documents** that you distribute during a workshop, on which the participants can make notes, so that they remain (inter)active throughout the presentation.

Of course, it is always possible that you will want to hand out other material: a prospectus, an annual report, back-up documents, etc.

SPEAKER NOTES

You base these notes on your storyline. They are the story of your presentation in telegram style. The notes can be in document form, on your crib cards or in the 'speaker notes' boxes of your software program.

In speaker notes you jot down only short points, not full sentences. (Complete sentences need to be 'read out', so you lose crucial eye contact with your audience.) You need little more than the key words you use to tell your story: 'story about banknote' is enough to jog your memory. Also add in practical 'stage directions', such as 'pause' or 'move to next slide'.

Don't follow the notes slavishly during your presentation; they are just reminders for your memory or prompts for when your inspiration dries up.

Presentation programs let you show speaker notes on the screen, next to your slides. This is great in theory but, in practice, often it is difficult to read the notes from the screen.

HANDOUTS

Depending on the type of presentation and your objectives, handouts make it possible for participants to restudy your key messages after the presentation, and to look more closely at some of the details.

Of course, your handout is not just a carbon copy of your powerpoint.

Its purpose is to make sure that the audience doesn't need to note things down during the presentation, so that it can focus on what you are saying. People are not made for multitasking. Without handouts, your audience would spend half the presentation scribbling down notes, missing part of your message as a result. Distribute your handout at the end rather than at the beginning; otherwise people will flick through it whilst you are speaking, and you will lose their attention.

You can make a handout easily by combining your speaker notes and slides in a text document. Programs like PowerPoint have an export function where one press of a button creates a text document out of your speaker notes, with the slides included as illustrations. With a few small text and layout adjustments, you can quickly transform this into the perfect handout.

WORK DOCUMENTS

As a general rule, you want to prevent people from looking at documents whilst you are talking. The single exception is when you want to turn your presentation into a work session. You can do this by building in specific moments when you give the participants the opportunity to take notes or fill in part of a work document. In this way, they will not be writing when you are speaking. Work documents can take many different forms, but avoid 'reading' documents that tempt your audience to flick through them in the middle of your presentation.

OTHER DOCUMENTS AND PRESENTATION MATERIAL

Don't present a new advertising campaign with a powerpoint. Instead, use prototypes of the posters, folders and other visual material. Likewise, if you are launching a website, just show it and surf through it. But make sure that you have an offline version on your computer, in case internet is not available. And, with product presentations, use the product itself as an aid. You can show its advantages much better with the real thing than with a powerpoint!

Conclusion? You don't always have to work with slides! You can do an entire presentation with a single poster. Or with crib cards that you later work into handout. For a small audience, show the real stuff rather than slides.

IN SHORT

In addition to your presentation, you may need other materials. These can be speaker notes, handouts and work documents. However you make your documents, make sure they don't interfere with the contact you, as speaker, have with your audience during the presentation.

Get ready!

Prepare to focus on your audience

David was my golf teacher. Sadly, he is no longer with us, but I learnt an awful lot from him. Every golfer will agree: golf is a really difficult sport. Every detail of your swing has an influence on the flight of the ball. The smallest thing can make the difference between the ball on the green and the ball in the lake. The way you hold the club, the position of your feet, the pressure of your hands on the grip, the opening of the club face, the angle of your upswing, the turn of your hips, the flexing of your knees, the power of your downswing, the breaking of your wrists, the coordination of all these different elements ... Everything needs to be right. Only then will that little white ball fly where you want it to go. 'And your swing also needs to feel natural,'' adds David. Natural? You've got to be joking! But he was right, of course.

That's why golfers practise so much. They spend hours hitting shot after shot, analysing each part of their swing with attention and patience. But, when they are out on the course, they no longer want to think about all these things. Instead, they are focused on their game and on their objective. They forget all the things they think about during practice and let their swing work naturally. And do you know what? It works!

It is just the same with a presentation. You need to prepare and practise. You need to think about all the different elements you must bring together if you want to achieve success. But, once you are standing in front of your audience, stop thinking about all that and focus fully on the interaction with your audience and your objective.

STEP 12
GET READY!

You are now at the end of your preparation. During your rehearsal you can still change the fine detail. But don't be tempted to change anything essential. You can keep on 'fine-tuning' till the cows come home, but there comes a moment when enough is enough. This is that moment. If you have carried out the preceding phases and actions correctly, nothing can go wrong. Run through the entire presentation at least once. The more lifelike your rehearsal, the more you will get out of it. So speak out loud and do it standing up. If you have an audience – your team, your boss, your partner – so much the better. Ask them to be your coach. Give them the following checklists and ask for honest feedback.

TALK NATURALLY

- **Use clear and simple language.** Talk like you normally do. Avoid jargon and formal expressions.

- **Repeat out loud the titles of your slides.** These should be short, powerful statements. Use exactly the same words as on the slides. This reduces cognitive load. Too many speakers say the same thing but with different words.

- **Learn the key sentences by heart.** Key sentences include your first sentence, your closing sentence and your key messages.

- **Speak in a conversational style**, using questions. You can either answer them yourself or let your audience do so. Either way, it increases interaction and focuses attention. Your pyramid is structured already in a question-and-answer format, so make use of it. Also use pauses for effect: 'Why should we change?' (pause). 'Well, there are three very good reasons. The first is ...'

- **Use forceful language.** Don't minimise your presentation by using weak language: 'This is a small example of what ...', 'A possible option might be ...', 'One of the proposals they could consider eventually is ...' This is not a good idea.

- **Speak loudly and clearly.** A voice you can hardly hear or understand demands a high cognitive effort from your audience.

- **Use a microphone.** If you are in a large room, ask for a microphone. If there is one, use it. Many presenters don't do this; they think it is more 'macho' without. They are wrong.

- **Insert pauses.** Do this just before or just after a key part of your presentation. This brings calm, strengthens your message, and gives people time to think about what you have said. It reduces the cognitive load and increases attention levels.

USE SIMPLE LANGUAGE

Back in Part I you read about the 'curse of knowledge'. We can never know for sure how our words will be received by someone who doesn't know what we know. So make sure you always use simple language. Avoid complex sentences, jargon, technotalk and grandiloquent words.

This will make your communication easier to understand and lower the (generative) cognitive load and your audience will have more cognitive energy available to absorb your message.

Technical jargon may, however, be used in the following limited circumstances:

- if technical terminology is more precise than ordinary language;
- if you know the audience is familiar with the technical terminology.

In all other cases, leave jargon well alone. I once heard a speaker say:

By redesigning a lean process that must lead to diminution of the current unnecessary level of bureaucratisation, we are going to improve the customer interface at our front office, so that we can react with vigour to the idiosyncratic demands of our customers.

Whilst what he meant was:

We are going to get rid of outdated rules and give our staff more freedom to deal with the needs of customers.

Another example?

Please note that the considerable downsizing and its related cost-reduction implications were made possible only by a change process that resulted in more efficient and more effective purchasing procedures.

Or does it sound better this way?

We have made savings by simplifying our buying procedures.

'Use simple language' really means 'speak like you normally speak'. But, for some strange reason, people often have the inclination to speak in 'formal' language when they are in an 'official' setting, like a presentation. As a summary, here are a few rules to remember:

1 **Avoid jargon.** The speaker understands the jargon; his audience usually does not.
2 **Speak with the audience.** Don't talk *about* your subject, but speak *with* the audience. Do not say: 'Research has shown ...' but say 'Take a look at the figures in this table ...'
3 **Use short sentences.** Sometimes you can lose control of long sentences. You know where they start, but you are never quite sure where they are going to end.

4 **Use concrete words.** Avoid nominalisation (the use of verbs or adjectives as nouns), such as 'Use solar panels for your house's heating'. It's better to say: 'Heat your house with solar panels.'

5 **Avoid the use of auxiliary verbs.** Avoid words like can, will, must … and other vague formulations. Don't say: 'In this table you can see …' Say: 'In this table you see …'

USE CONCRETE, ILLUSTRATIVE LANGUAGE

As well as using simple language without jargon, you need to consider the use of illustrative, image-rich language. These are your mini 'handles'. Educational scientists know that, for children in primary school, 'Calculate $3 \times 4 + 5 - 2 = …$' is a much more difficult task than, 'On the playground there are three groups of four children. Later on, five other children join them and two children leave. How many children are there left on the playground?'

What is concrete? The following examples speak for themselves:

ABSTRACT (VAGUE) LANGUAGE	CONCRETE LANGUAGE
A powerful motor	A 6 cylinder with 300 hp
A high dose	2000 mg per day
A long flight	A 9-hour flight
Less sugar	Less than 0.7 g sugar per 100 g
Longer life-expectancy	Living three years longer

And free yourself from your slides:

- **Don't make yourself dependent on your slides.** Don't use your slides as memory aids. You should look at them only to make something clear to your audience.

- **Introduce your slides.** Many speakers click first on the slide, look at what it says, and then begin with the explanation: 'As you can see on the slide, the market has grown less quickly than we thought …' It is much better to announce your slide and its content before you click on it: 'The market has grown much less quickly than we thought. Let's look at the following slide, which shows …'

ADOPT A NATURAL POSTURE, CLOSE TO THE AUDIENCE

- **Always stand.** Even in smaller meetings. After all, you are giving a presentation!
- **Be aware of your posture.** You know what makes you feel comfortable, so adopt that position. Make yourself big. Don't slouch. Avoid everything that makes you uncertain or gives an uncertain impression: rocking on one leg, fingering your collar, playing with your glasses, etc.
- **Dare to use your hands** or keep them calmly at your side. Holding a pointer or your notes sometimes can help. Don't fidget.
- **Give your presentation as though you were doing it for friends.**
- **Move!** Don't hide behind a desk or lectern. And don't stay rooted to a single spot. Move about and don't be afraid to stand close to your audience, since this increases connection. If possible, move amongst the audience (for example, if there is a central aisle).

SHOW AN OPEN AND POSITIVE ATTITUDE

- **First and foremost, be yourself.**
- **Be enthusiastic.** Enthusiasm is contagious. Even if your audience doesn't respond, remain enthusiastic yourself.
- **Dare to make mistakes.** If you stumble over your words, say sorry and just carry on – like you would in a normal conversation.
- **Ask for feedback from the audience.** 'What do you think? Do you agree?'
- **Don't apologise for your so-called 'weaknesses'.** Many speakers begin by apologising for their slides, their lack of preparation, their nerves, etc. Don't do it! What you think are weaknesses almost always pass by your audience unnoticed – unless you point them out.

MAKE CONTACT WITH YOUR AUDIENCE

- **Make eye contact.** Look at individuals in the audience like you would look at a friend when you are pouring him a glass of wine.
- **Don't be afraid of questions.** They are a sign of interest.
- **Invite your audience to ask questions.** Plan specific moments during your presentation when the audience can ask questions. Announce this at the start, so that people can focus fully on you when you are talking.

STEP 12
GET READY!

- **Rephrase questions in your own words.** In this way, you can check if you have understood the question correctly and make the question clear for everyone in the audience. It also gives you time to think of an answer!

- **If necessary, win thinking time by asking for clarification.** 'Do you mean ...?' Or explain why you would prefer to leave the answer to that particular question until later on. No one expects you to know everything.

CHECK YOUR EQUIPMENT

Check all your equipment and technical aids. If possible, hold a general rehearsal at the venue, so that you can test everything 'live'. Does the powerpoint work the way you planned? Are there gaps? Do the slide transfers work well? Is the synchronisation okay? If you are worrying about these things during your presentation, you won't be able to focus fully on your audience and your message. In practice, this means:

- **Test the software.** There are different versions of PowerPoint and other software packages. This can affect your presentation. Check that everything works well on the equipment you use.

- **Use a wireless pointer.** This allows you to move backwards and forwards during your presentation. Make sure you know how it works.

- **Test the screen and the projector**, with the same lighting you will use on the day. Is everything legible? Will the bottom of the screen be visible when the room is full of people? Go to the back of the room and check.

- **Test the sound** and the microphone.

- **Test all the technical equipment** you will use, such as videos, online connections, etc.

- **Make concrete arrangements** with the event manager or the technical staff.

- **If you use a screen with speaker notes, check that it is properly placed.**

Also, you can make a checklist for the day of the presentation. Run through it just before you start or ask someone else to do it for you. Check that everything is in order – and then forget about it. It's too late to change anything now. Relax, and give it your best shot. It will all be okay!

Take time to have a chat with your audience before the meeting. You are well-prepared and confident – so let them see it. And, even if all your equipment lets you down, you have your pyramid structure still in your head and your list of handles. They are enough to get your key message across – and to achieve your objective.

IN SHORT

You are ready to go. After rehearsing, testing all your equipment and running through your checklist for a final time, there is only one thing left to do. Be yourself. Take a deep breath, stand up, focus on your audience and go for it! Good luck!

'In order to make a good speech:
*First: **stand up**, so that you can be seen.*
*Then: **speak up**, so that you can be heard.*
*And then: **shut up**, in order to stay interesting!'*

Professor Dr J.A. Gruwez

What did you think of this book?

We're really keen to hear from you about this book, so that we can make our publishing even better.

Please log on to the following website and leave us your feedback.

It will only take a few minutes and your thoughts are invaluable to us.

www.pearsoned.co.uk/bookfeedback

STEP 12
GET READY!

Conclusion

The design process of your presentation is now complete. It is a thorough process that allows you to make excellent presentations. Even if you don't have much time, the basic structure of the process will help you still. Focus on each of the four phases:

Remember that Phase 1 is the most important and Phase 4 the least important. Form without content is useless. And, if you don't know who your audience is and what your objectives are, your content is useless as well.

It is also important to remember the principles of the working memory:

- Ask for, and hold, your audience's attention.

- Make your message easy to understand by limiting its cognitive load.

- Fix your message in your audience's mind through repetition, stories and the use of sensory detail.

To help you with all these things, you can download checklists from my website as well as a summary poster of the design process. You can use this to refresh your own memory or as a guide for your next presentation. And, of course, this book is also your friend and ally. Return to it whenever you begin a new presentation.

I hope that it will help you to raise your presentations to a higher level; that you will achieve better results with less effort; and that your audience will be surprised by just how clear and entertaining your presentations have become!

Good luck and thank you for your interest.

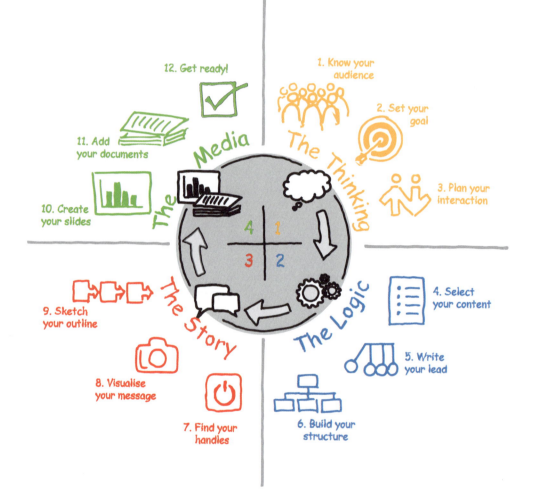

Appendix: The TLSM method at a glance

THE TLSM METHOD IN 4 PHASES

Phase 1: The Thinking

Take a step back and look at the bigger picture. Find somewhere quiet and take time to think about the essence of your presentation. Why should they listen to you? What do you want to achieve? How are you going to achieve it?

Phase 2: The Logic

Before you start to develop your story, first you need to fix the objective content of your presentation. Think logically. What are you going to talk about? More importantly, what are you not going to talk about? What is the key of your argument? Are all your ideas logically connected? How can you structure these ideas so that they can be understood easily?

Phase 3: The Story

Now that you have fixed the objective content of your presentation, you can start to write your story. This requires a more creative approach. You must encapsulate your message in a slick story: appealing and memorable.

Phase 4: The Media

Your story is ready. In this final phase you now need to find the best way to implement it. This involves making slides and preparing documents that support your key message. Double-check everything to make sure that it all goes smoothly on the day. If you have done the previous three phases properly, this should be a piece of cake.

THE TLSM METHOD IN 12 STEPS

Step 1: Know your audience

Why should they listen to you?

Knowing your audience – understanding their feelings and emotions – is the most important thing of all. Contact the organiser of the presentation. Ask what they know already and what they expect. Ask for advice and guidance.

If you have more time:

- Find out who the key figures and opinion makers are. Ask all the essential questions about these people. Make sure you know what your audience knows and thinks about the subject of your presentation. In this way, you can build on solid ground.

- Arrange with your supporters in the audience how they will support you. But also talk to your opponents, so that you really understand what they think.

Step 2: Set your goal

What do you want to achieve?

Write down the answers to the following two questions:

- When will I regard my presentation as successful? In other words, what do I want to achieve?

- If I want my audience to remember just one thing, what should that be? In other words, what is my key message?

If you have more time:

- Describe your objective in terms of information, action and emotion. What do you want your audience to know, do and feel?

- Try to find a powerful one-liner, perhaps as a metaphor, to ram home your key message.

- If you end up with several key messages, think about splitting the subject into more than one presentation.

- If you can't find a good key message, you get a second chance to do this in Step 5.

Step 3: Plan your interaction

How do you want to achieve your objective?

Decide how you want to interact with your audience to achieve your objective. How much time do you have? Are you going to work with slides or not? What opportunities do the venue and the size of the group offer?

If you have more time:

- Make sure you have a clear strategy for interaction.
- A number of elements need to be defined and coordinated, such as:
  - the type of meeting;
  - the size of the group;
  - the location;
  - the timing;
  - necessary prior knowledge;
  - printed pre- and post-documentation.

Step 4: Select the content

Scrap the irrelevant, keep the essential

Decide what needs to be included in your presentation. Limit yourself to things that support your key message and bring you closer to your objective. Be critical. Is everything you have chosen really necessary? The shorter your list, the more memorable your story will be.

If you have more time:

- First you can draw up a longlist, containing as many ideas and arguments as you can.
- Then this longist can be whittled down to a shortlist, by removing everything that does not bring you nearer to your objective. Remember that too many arguments and choice options always have a negative impact on your presentation.

Step 5: Write your lead

Begin with your conclusion

This is the core of your presentation. It is your executive summary:

- Outline the situation (background) briefly – the things everyone already knows and agrees with.
- What issue will you solve and what question does that issue raise?
- What is your answer to this question? That is your key message.

If you have more time:

- This is the most important part of your presentation, so make sure you get it right! Do the situation, complication, question and answer (key message) all support your objective in a balanced manner?
- Make the complication, question and key message as short and precise as possible.

Step 6: Build your structure

Create an impeccable, scalable logic

Map your ideas in a pyramid structure, with your key message at the top. Make sure your ideas are grouped logically, with three to seven arguments per group, summarised with a strong assertion.

If you have more time:

- Apply the Minto Principles to your pyramid structure.
- Start at the top with your key message. Ask a question that is induced by that assertion and give different answers to that question. For each of those answers, ask a new question that yields different assertions as an answer. And so on.
- Check if your pyramid complies with the laws of logical communication and minimal cognitive load:
    - There is an assertion or a proposition in each box, not just a word.
    - Working from top to bottom, the map reads like a question-and-answer conversation.
    - Working from bottom to top, each group of assertions forms one or more arguments that are summarised in a more abstract overarching assertion or conclusion.
    - At the highest level, only inductive logic is used.
    - All the groups of assertions are exclusive and exhaustive.
    - Each group of assertions is listed in a clear order, reflecting the logic of the grouping.
- Delete, refine and amend your map until it forms a coherent whole.
- This is probably the most difficult part of the entire book.

Step 7: Find your handles

Colour your message

Handles are like buttons that you need to press to attract people's attention, clarify your message and plant it firmly in the memory of those listening. Try to find at least one handle, perhaps an anecdote, that will grab the attention of your audience.

If you have more time:

- Search for further handles that will stimulate the brain's response.
- Possible handles include: images, examples, anecdotal stories, analogies and metaphors, surprise elements, emotions, quotes, experiences, questions, humour, facts and figures.
- Think carefully about the possible effect of your handles. This effect must be positive and must make the connection with your key message.
- Insert your handles at strategic points in your pyramid structure. Distribute them evenly throughout the presentation, so that you can hold your audience's attention.

Step 8: Visualise your message

Use 'sticky' images

Images are the most powerful handles. Find or make a strong image (photo or figure) that visually strengthens your key message and/or clarifies the structure of your story. Make sure that this image is identified with your presentation.

If you have more time:

- Create a number of key visuals that support or illustrate your key message:
  - Photos that generate feelings and emotions.
  - Figures and diagrams that illustrate and/or enhance your key message.
- Make sure these images actually clarify what you are trying to say. They must support your message; otherwise, they will simply attract attention away from it.

Step 9: Sketch your outline

Find a natural flow

This shouldn't take long. Use your lead as your introduction, then work through your pyramid structure from top to bottom (as a kind of question-and-answer conversation), adding in handles at regular intervals. Tack on a short ending – and Bob's your uncle! That's all there is to it: your story is ready. You don't even need to write it down. Just make sure that you learn the first and last sentences by heart.

If you have more time:

- Write down your story in a series of bullet points. You need write out only the most important sentences in full; in particular, the beginning and the ending. Use simple, concrete language. Avoid jargon.

- The structure of your story should look like this:
  - **Introduction = the lead**
    - Add a strong handle so that you grab people's attention right from the start. By playing with the order of the situation, complication and answer (key message), it is possible to create different sensations in your presentation.
  - **Middle**
    - Use your pyramid structure, sprinkled with handles.
    - Work from top to bottom of the pyramid.
    - Before moving from one step to another, come back to the higher level of abstraction, so that your audience doesn't lose the thread of your argument.
  - **End**
    - Make the end short and to the point. Ask for commitment and use emotion to underscore your key message. Alternatively, frame your key message in a more philosophical perspective.
    - Make sure that your closing text can be added at various positions in your presentation, just in case you run short of time.

Step 10: Create your slides

Keep it minimal

If time is tight, you can make minimalist slides or even none at all. If need be, you can draw diagrams on a flip chart during the presentation. If you have the time to make slides, be sure they actually support and clarify your story. Whatever your preferred method, simplicity is crucial.

If you have more time:

- Design your slides first on paper; this will focus your attention on the content and the subject, rather than on the technical gimmicks of the software.

- When designing your slides, make sure you keep the cognitive load for your audience to a minimum; this allows them to devote their full attention to absorbing your message rather than trying to decipher your slides.

Step 11: Add your documents

Repeat your key message

Not enough time? Then work without supporting documents. Use the pyramid structure as your own presentation guide.

If you have more time:
- Prepare the following documents, if appropriate:
  - Clear, short speaker notes for yourself, so that you don't need to read constantly from your slides.
  - A handout for your public that summarises the most important aspects of the presentation.
  - If desired, a work document that will allow you to involve the audience more actively during the presentation.

Step 12: Get ready!

Prepare to focus on your audience

Your presentation is done and dusted. Check that it is well-matched to your objective, audience and setting, as detailed in Phase 1. If it is, you can start practising and fine-tuning. Check that your logistical tools are all working properly. No problems? Then you are ready to concentrate fully on your audience.

If you have more time:
- Practise the presentation in a setting that closely resembles the actual venue.
- Ask someone to give feedback about your style of presenting. But resist the temptation to tamper too much with your story at the last moment.
- Use a natural way of speaking, a relaxed approach and a normal posture, so that you can maintain maximum contact with your public.
- Double-check all the technical and logistical aspects. Make a checklist to be certain that you don't forget anything.

Further reading and references

These are the references cited in the book. For further references and interesting reading please refer to **www.edgruwez.com**.

PART I – A BETTER UNDERSTANDING OF PRESENTATIONS

Atkinson, R.C. and Shiffrin, R.M., 'Human memory: a proposed system and its control processes' in Spence, K.W. and Spence, J.T. (1968) *The Psychology of Learning and Motivation 2*. Academic Press, pp. 89–195.

Baddeley, A., 'Working memory', *Science*, 255(5044) (1992), pp. 556–59.

Baddeley, A.D. and Hitch, G.J., 'Developments in the concept of working memory', *Neuropsychology*, 8(4) (1994), pp. 485–93.

Baddeley, A.D., 'Working memory: the interface between memory and cognition' in Gazzaniga, M.S. (ed.) (2000) *Cognitive Neuroscience: A Reader*. Malden, MA: Blackwell.

Barrett, L.F., Tugade, M.M. and Engle, R.W., 'Individual differences in working memory capacity and dual-process theories of the mind', *Psychological Bulletin*, 130 (2004), pp. 553–73.

Buchholz, A., 'The call of solitude', *Psychology Today*, 31(1) (1998), pp. 50–54.

Bumiller, E., 'We have met the enemy and he is PowerPoint', *The New York Times*, 26 April 2010.

Casteleyn, J. (2013) *New Media and the Rhethoric of Presentations: Explorations in Education*. Academia Press.

Covey, S.R. (2004) *The 7 Habits of Highly Effective People: Powerful Lessons in Personal Change*. London: Simon & Schuster.

Cowan, N., 'The magical number 4 in short-term memory: a reconsideration of mental storage capacity', *Behavioral and Brain Sciences*, 24 (2000), pp. 87–185.

Cowan, N., Zhijian, C. and Rouder, J.N., 'Constant capacity in an immediate serial-recall task: a logical sequel to Miller (1956)', *Psychological Science*, 15(9) (2004), pp. 634–40.

Gruwez, E. and Vanseer, K., 'The economic impact of presentations', 7 April 2014, www.tothepointatwork.com

Heath, C. and Heath, D., 'The curse of knowledge', *Harvard Business Review* (Dec. 2006).

Heath, C. and Heath, D. (2007) *Made to Stick: Why Some Ideas Survive and Others Die*. New York, NY: Random House.

Hitch, G.J., 'Temporal grouping effects in immediate recall: a working memory analysis', *The Quarterly Journal of Experimental Psychology Section A: Human Experimental Psychology*, 49(1) (1996), pp. 116–39.

Kaplan, S., 'Strategy and PowerPoint: an inquiry into the epistemic culture and machinery of strategy making', *Organisation Sciences*, 22(2) (2011), pp. 320–46.

Mayer, R. (2009) *Multimedia Learning*, 2nd edn. New York: Cambridge University Press.

Medina, J. (2008) *Brain Rules. 12 Principles for Surviving and Thriving at Work, Home and School*. Seattle: Pear Press.

Miller, G.A., 'The magical number seven, plus or minus two: some limits on our capacity for processing information', P*sychological Review*, 63 (1956), pp. 81–97.

Newton, L., 'Overconfidence in the Communication of Intent: Heard and Unheard Melodies', Ph.D. dissertation (1990), Stanford University.

Norman, D., 'In defence of PowerPoint' (2004), retrieved from: http://www.jnd.org/dn.mss/in_defense_of_powerp.html

Repovs, G. and Baddeley, A., 'The multi-component model of working memory: explorations in experimental cognitive psychology, *Neuroscience*, 139 (2006), pp. 5–21.

Reynolds, G. (2008) *Presentation Zen: Simple Ideas on Presentation Design and Delivery*. Berkeley, CA: New Riders.

Sinek, S. (2009) *Start with Why: How Great Leaders Inspire Everyone to Take Action*. London: Penguin.

PART II – BUILDING YOUR PRESENTATION

Phase 1 – The Thinking

Covey, S.R. (2004) *The 7 Habits of Highly Effective People: Powerful Lessons in Personal Change*. London: Simon & Schuster.

Godden, D.R. and Baddeley, A.D., 'Context-dependent memory in two natural environments: on land and underwater', *British Journal of Psychology*, 66(3) (1975), pp. 325–32.

Heath, C. and Heath, D. (2007) *Made to Stick: Why Some Ideas Survive and Others Die*. New York, NY: Random House.

Herrmann, N. (1996) *The Whole Brain Business Book: Unlocking the Power of Whole Brain Thinking in Organisations and Individuals*. New York, NY: McGraw-Hill.

Lencioni, P. (2004) *Death by Meeting: A Leadership Fable About Solving the Most Painful Problem in Business*. San Francisco, CA: Jossey-Bass.

Mayer, R. (2009) *Multimedia Learning*, 2nd edn. New York: Cambridge University Press.

Reynolds, G. (2008) *Presentation Zen: Simple Ideas on Presentation Design and Delivery*. Berkeley, CA: New Riders.

Simmons, A. (2007) *Whoever Tells the Best Story Wins: How to Use Your Own Stories to Communicate with Power and Impact*. New York: American Management Association.

Sinek, S. (2009) *Start with Why: How Great Leaders Inspire Everyone to Take Action*. London: Penguin.

Phase 2 – The Logic

Buzan, T. and Buzan, B. (1993) *The Mindmap Book*. London, UK: BBC Books.

Cialdini, R.B. (2000) *Influence: Science and Practice*. New York, NY: Pearson Education.

Cooper, G. (1998) *Research into Cognitive Load Theory and Instructional Design at UNSW*. Sydney, Australia: University of New South Wales.

Hitch, G.J., 'Temporal grouping effects in immediate recall: a working memory analysis', *The Quarterly Journal of Experimental Psychology Section A: Human Experimental Psychology*, 49(1) (1996), pp. 116–39.

Minto, B. (1981) *The Pyramid Principle: Logic in Writing and Thinking*, 3rd edn. Harlow, UK: FT-Prentice Hall.

Rasiel, E. (1999) *The McKinsey Way*, 1st edn. New York, NY: McGraw-Hill.

Redelmeier, D.A. and Shafir, E., 'Medical decision making in situations that offer multiple alternatives', *Journal of the American Medical Association*, 273 (1995), pp. 302–6.

Tversky, A. and Shafir, E., 'The disjunction effect in choice under uncertainty', *Psychological Science*, (1992), pp. 305–9.

Phase 3 – The Story

Baddeley, A., 'The episodic buffer: a new component of working memory?', *Trends in Cognitive Sciences*, 4(11) (2000), pp. 417–23.

Bensabat, I. and Dexter, A.S., 'An experimental evaluation of graphical and color-enhanced information presentation', *Management Science*, 31(11) (1985), pp. 1348–64.

Brosch, T., et al., 'The impact of emotion on perception, attention, memory, and decision-making', *Swiss Medical Weekly* (14 May 2013).

Fenton-O'Creevy, M., et al., 'Thinking, feeling and deciding: The influence of emotions on the decision making and performance of traders', *Journal of Organizational Behavior*, 32(8) (Nov. 2010), pp. 1044–61.

Heath, C. and Heath, D. (2007) *Made to Stick: Why Some Ideas Survive and Others Die*. New York, NY: Random House.

Heilman, R.M. and Liviu, G.C., 'Emotion regulation and decision making under risk and uncertainty', *Emotion*, 10(2), American Psychology Association (2010), pp. 257–65.

Kensinger, E.A., 'Remembering the details: effects of emotion', *Emotion Review*, 1(2) (April 2009), pp. 99–113.

Lencioni, P.M. (2002) *The Five Dysfunctions of a Team: A Leadership Fable*. San Francisco, CA: Jossey-Bass.

Mayer, R. (2009) *Multimedia Learning*, 2nd edn. New York: Cambridge University Press.

Medina, J. (2008). *Brain Rules. 12 Principles for Surviving and Thriving at Work, Home and School*. Seattle: Pear Press.

Rossiter, J.R. and Percy, L., 'Attitude change through visual imagery in advertising', *Journal of Advertising*, 9(2) (1980), pp. 107–11.

Shafir, E., Simonson, I. and Tversky, A., 'Reason-based choice', *Cognition*, 19 (1993), pp. 11–36

Simmons, A. (2007) *Whoever Tells the Best Story Wins: How to Use Your Own Stories to Communicate with Power and Impact*. New York: American Management Association.

Phase 4 – The Media

Mayer, R. (2009) *Multimedia Learning*, 2nd edn. New York: Cambridge University Press.

Meyers-Levy, J. and Perracchio, A., 'Understanding the effects of color: how the correspondence between available and required resources affects attitudes', *Journal of Consumer Research*, 22(2) (Sep. 1995), pp. 121–138

Norman, D., 'In defence of PowerPoint' (2004), retrieved from: http://www.jnd.org/dn.mss/in_defense_of_powerp.html

Smits, T. (2013) *When to Discolour Your Message: The Relative Persuasive Power of Black-and-White Imagery.* Not yet published, draft text received from the author.

Index

communication *(continued)*
    and the working memory 23
companies, presentation culture 13
complex information, for knowledgeable audience 76–7
complication
    as element of a lead 93–4
    in introduction 149–51
conclusion
    flexible 154–5
    starting with 89–91
    too late 12
Confucius 134
conscious attention 120
consequences of bad presentations 7–8
consistency and commitment 81
content
    bad 13
    lack of 13
    logic and story 74–5
    preparation of presentations xiii
    selection 97–116, 209
'Contiguity Principle' 192
converging phase 79, 83–8
conversation
    style of talking 198
    through pyramid structure 116
Cooper, Graham 76
counter-arguments in shortlist 83
Covey, Stephen 48
creative thinking 18–20

Das Auto 60
data visualisation 140, 166, 189–91
De Pelsmaker, Johan xi
De Wilde, Mr 47
decision making
    emotions 131–3
    methods 82–3
    number of options 84–5
    visual representation 141–2
decorative elements on slides 28–9, 146
decrease, visual representation 145
deductive reasoning 107
design
    process for presentations 21, 34–41
    slides *see* slides: design
details, too many 12
Dexter, A.S. 140
diagrams 141, 186–7, 189–91, 211
digital-analogue-digital slide design 168–70

dimensions in longlist 81
diverging phase 79–83
division of presentation, for maintaining attention 136, 158
Django Unchained (film) 134
documents, additional 193–6, 212–13
dual channel approach 26–8
duration *see* time

Einstein, Albert 77
elaborate encoding 123
electronic interaction 71–2
emotions
    audience commitment 50–1, 58–9
    balance with reason xiii
    in conclusion 155
    as handles 129–33
    impact 32–3
    importance 75
empathic listening 48
enthusiasm for subject 19
environment, importance of 67–8
Epictetus 47
episodic memory 126
equipment check 202
essential information 79
examples as handles 124
executive memory 25, 38–9, 119–20
eye contact 6, 66, 201

famous stories as handles 125
feedback 6, 11, 198, 201, 213
feelings *see* emotions
Fenton-O'Creevy, Mark 132
figures 135–6, 141, 211
first impressions 89–90, 151
Five Dysfunctions of a Team, The (Lencioni) 131
flip charts for visual support 69, 80, 162, 167, 212
focusing on the audience 197–8
fonts and sizes for text on slides 181
four-phase design method *see* TLSM method
functional magnetic resonance imaging (fMRI) 130

General Electric 53
General Motors 5, 55
get ready *see* preparation: final
goals and objectives
    in conclusion 154–5
    importance 45–6
    setting 55–62, 208

Lencioni, Patrick 64, 131
length of presentation, excessive 12
liking, use of 81
limitations, making the most of 19
limited capacity of working memory 28–30
listening
    empathic 48
    importance 47–8
location, importance 63–4, 66–8
logic
    defined 74
    focus on xiii
    importance 75
    in pyramid structure levels 113–14
Logic phase 36–7, 73–116, 207
    building the structure 97–116
    content
        importance 73–7
        selecting 78–88
    writing the lead 89–96
logical content, before story content 74–5
logical structure, reason for 97–8
London Business School xi
London Stock Exchange 132–3
longlist, drawing up a 79–83
long-term memory
    and the brain 151
    and episodic memory 126
    and impact of emotions 32–3
    and importance of repetition 153–4
    and TLSM method 38–9
    and working memory 25–6

Mackiewicz 164
manipulation 81
Mayer, Richard 23, 34, 58, 139, 145, 176, 180, 185, 192
McChrystal, General Stanley 14
McCloskey, Robert 11, 12
McGregor, Ewan 138
McGurk Effect 70–1, 123, 138
McKinsey Way, The (Raisel) 112
measurement, visual representation 142
MECE (mutually exclusive and collectively exhaustive)
            principle 112–13
media naturalness 6, 70–1
Media phase 36–7, 161–203, 207
    adding documents 193–6
    creating slides 163–92
        choice of visual tools 161–3
        graphic design 175–92

making slides 167–72
using templates 173–4
visualisation of story 163–6
final preparation 197–203
Medina, John 23, 148, 151, 158
medium, choice of for visual support 161–3
meeting slides 165
meeting type, importance 64
memory
    cognitive 129–30
    episodic 126
    executive 25, 38–9, 119–20
    grouping for recall 101
    impact of emotions 32–3, 129–30
    importance of repetition 153–4
    and location 67–8
    long-term 25–6, 32–3, 38–9, 126, 151, 153–4
    recognising 25, 26–8, 38–9, 119–20
    sensory 24, 38–9, 120
    and TLSM method 38–9
    working
        and attention 119–20
        and the brain 151
        and episodic memory 126
        handles to ensure penetration 121–3
        misconceptions 26–31
        principles of the 205
        theory of the 23–6
        and TLSM method 38–9
message
    importance of simplicity 75–7
    key
        as element of a lead 94–5
        in pyramid structure 102–3
        writing a 60–2
    unclear 12
    visualisation 138–47, 211
metaphors
    as handles 127
    in key message 61
Meyers-Levy, J. 185
middle of a presentation 152–4
Miller, George A. 23, 28
mindmaps 99
Minto, Barbara 92, 99, 100, 112
Minto International 92
misconceptions, in understanding audience 26–31
mistakes
    fear of 19
    in preparing presentations 12–16

Do you want your people to be the very best at what they do?

Talk to us about how we can help.

As the world's leading learning company, we know a lot about what your people need in order to be better at what they do.

Whatever subject or skills you've got in mind (from presenting or persuasion to coaching or communication skills), and at whatever level (from new-starters through to top executives) we can help you deliver tried-and-tested, essential learning straight to your workforce – whatever they need, whenever they need it and wherever they are.

Talk to us today about how we can:

- Complement and support your existing learning and development programmes
- Enhance and augment your people's learning experience
- Match your needs to the best of our content
- Customise, brand and change it to make a better fit
- Deliver cost-effective, great value learning content that's proven to work.

Contact us today:
corporate.enquiries@pearson.com

ALWAYS LEARNING